贾克德工笔花鸟画集

Flower — and — Bird Paintings of Jia Kede

走向“天人合一”之境

潘絜兹

中国画有个好传统，就是借物抒情。花鸟画在再现自然美之外，更需求写意传情，做到形神兼备。一个鸟语花香的世界是人类的理想，也是花鸟画家的天国。

在画家眼中，万物有情，一切景语皆情语。为了传情，不惜形似有先，追求似与不似之间的高境界，这是写意花鸟画的由来。对工笔花鸟画来说，要求以形传神，不是求标本式的眞实，而是千笔万笔皆写意，毫厘之间见精神。工写殊途同归，都是借物抒情。这是中国花鸟画的特点。

中国画的最高境界是天人合一，天就是大自然，宇宙规律。天生我，生万物，一切生命体都是有情物，所以我们的星球才生机活泼，才有人类这万物之灵，也才有艺术。中国画家所说的天人合一，就是主客观统一，情景相生，物我两忘。这个境界是难达到的；那些心中无物，信笔涂鸦，但求笔墨趣味的写意画，和但求眞实，规规形似，见物不见人的工笔画，都离这个境界很远。

是否可以归结为一点，中国的花鸟画是人化的自然，是自然物的超越。不入情就是死画，至多只是能品，妙品，不能称神品，更和逸品无缘。但是对工笔花鸟画来说，我不提逸品的要求，因为我认为一放逸就会使花鸟之美受到破坏和损害。一些工笔花鸟画家问我，工笔花鸟画如何出新？我说：“当人来画。”1983年我画了一套《花与女》组画，就想继承中国画借物抒情的优良传统，为工笔花鸟画的发展开拓新思路，创造新境界。但我限于能力，只是一种尝试，希望能有助于花鸟画家的创新实践而已。

贾克德是当代卓越的工笔花鸟画家，有浑厚的传统修养，又有扎实的写生能力，正和我同走在工笔复兴的道路上，致力于开拓创新，已取得了可喜的成就。他的工笔花鸟画，已超越传统模式，有自己的创新。他笔下的花鸟，不离自身的生态环境，不失自然的美，也注入了自己的情。他画所见，更重所感。如他所画枝头群雀，就像一群活泼可爱的孩子在嬉闹，是鸟也似人。人有情，花鸟亦有情，而且与人相通。杜甫诗“感时花溅泪，恨别鸟惊心”，正说出了中国花鸟画的特点，也是它的精髓所在；能掌握它，就能不翼而飞，出神入化，达到天人合一，由能品，进入妙品、神品了。

克德同志画集即将出版之际，我高兴地为他写序，作为祝贺。

Toward a Mental State of "Heaven and Man Being One"

by Pan Jiezi

The Chinese painting has a fine tradition: to express one's feelings through natural objects. The flower-and-bird painters strive to display the beauty of nature and at the same time human sentiments in harmony. A place where birds chirp and flowers emit fragrance is an ideal place for every one. It is also a paradise of flower-and-bird painters.

In the eye of the painter, every thing in the world has feelings and every natural object can speak. The painter may sacrifice the true form of an object in order to obtain a higher state which lingers between likeness and unlikeness. This is the origin of the flower-and-bird painting of freehand brushwork.

The meticulous brushwork requires to express the feelings through forms. But it does not require to copy the forms rigidly. Every stroke of the brush should express a certain meaning.

Both meticulous brushwork and freehand brushwork mean to express feelings through real things. This is the main characteristic of the Chinese flower-and-bird painting.

The highest state of mind of traditional Chinese painting is "Heaven and Man Being One". Here Heaven means the Nature, the law of the universe. According to Chinese ancient philosophy the Heaven gave birth to Man and everything in the world. All living things have feelings. This is why our earth is lively and there are human beings who have created arts.

For Chinese painters the philosophy of "Heaven and Man Being One" is the unification of the subjective world and the objective world, the mutual complement of sentiments and natural sights, and the total oblivion of oneself and the world. It is very difficult to achieve such a state of mind. Those painters of freehand brushwork who have no real knowledge, who paint at random, who only want to display skillful brush strokes are far from this state of mind; those painters of meticulous brushwork who only try to be truthful to real things and can see only forms but not feelings are far from such a state of mind too.

To summarize, Chinese flower-and-bird painting is to humanize the Nature and transcend natural things. Paintings without feelings are dead paintings. At most they can be regarded as capable paintings, excellent paintings, but not divine paintings, or superb paintings. Here I do not mean painters of meticulous brushwork all should produce superb paintings. If a painter is too carefree the beauty of birds, flowers and plants will be damaged. Some painters of meticulous brushwork asked me how they could achieve breakthroughs. I said: " To paint as if the things were human beings."

I painted a set of " Flowers and Women" in 1983 in the hope to blaze a new trail in flower-and-bird painting of meticulous brushwork by adhering to the fine tradition of Chinese painting: " To express feelings through real objects." Due to my limited abilities this was only a trial. I hope my practice may be useful to other flower-and-bird painters.

Jia Kede is an outstanding flower-and-bird painter of meticulous brushwork. He is well learned in traditional culture and highly skilled in sketching from real life. He and I are on the same road to invigorate the painting of meticulous brushwork and have made some inspiring results. His paintings have broken away from some traditional forms. The birds, flowers and plants he paints in natural environment display their natural beauty and express his feelings at the same time. The beholder can feel more about the painter's sentiments than see the real objects. The sparrows in his paintings are like young children playing. They give the beholder the feeling that the birds are also human beings. One of Du Fu's poems reads: " Blossoms invite my tears as in wild times they bloom; The flitting birds stir my heart as I'm parted from home." The words are an annotation of the characteristic of Chinese flower-and-bird painting. When the painter can master this characteristic he will be able to fly without wings, to reach the state of mind of " Heaven and Man Being One ", and can produce excellent and divine works.
I am very happy to write these words as a foreword to the *Selected Paintings of Jia Kede* and here I extend to him my congratulations.

First edition 1997

Published by China Esperanto Press, Beijing
24 Baiwanzhuang, Beijing, China
P.O.Box 77, Post code: 100037
Distributed by China International Book Trading
Corporation (Guojishudian)
35 W. Chegongzhuang Xilu, Beijing, China
P.O. Box 399, Post code: 100044

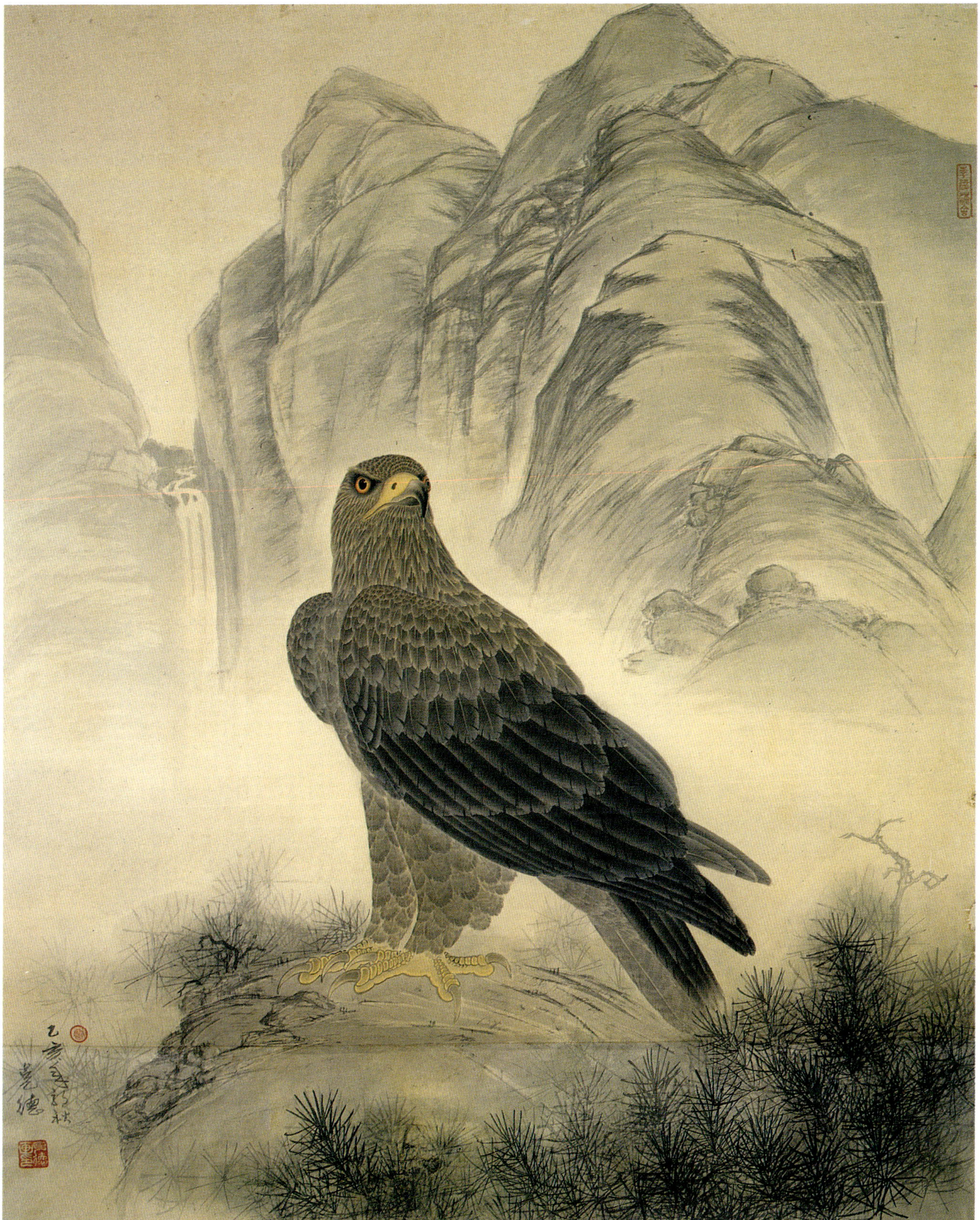

志当高远（1995） 绢本

High Aspirations

120 × 180cm (1995) on silk

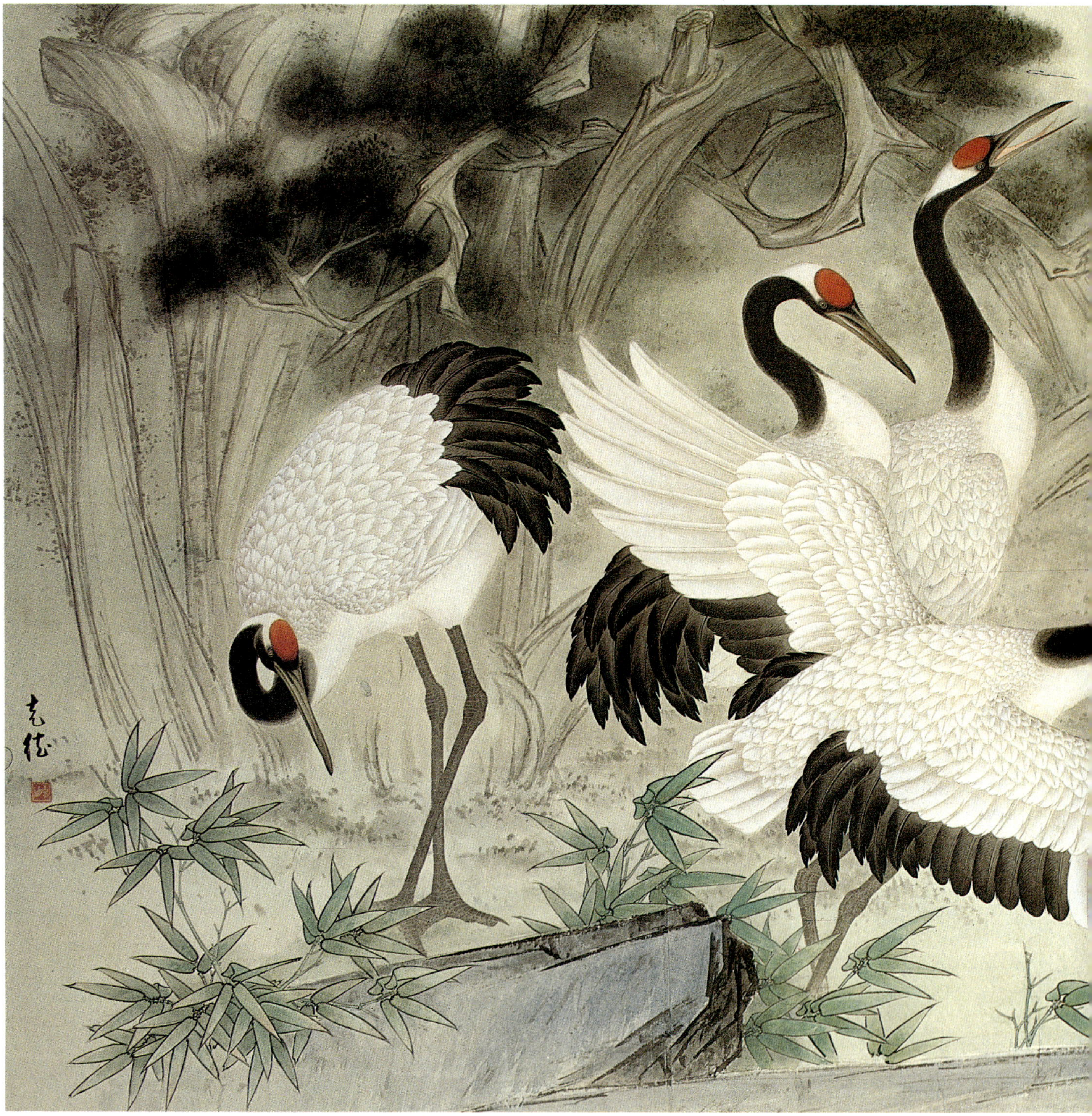

陆 鹤 图（1982） 绢本
Cranes
240 × 120cm (1982) on silk

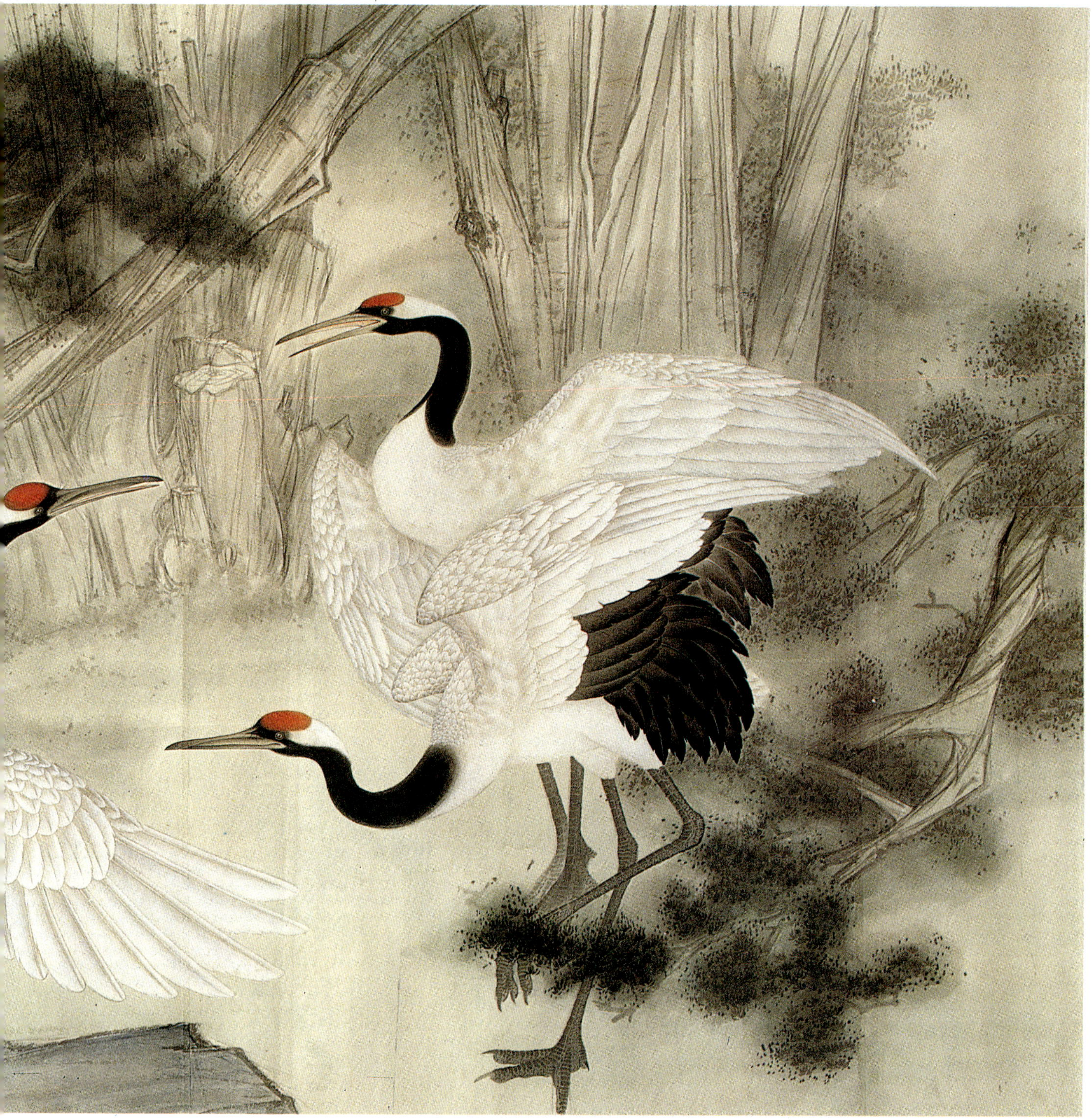

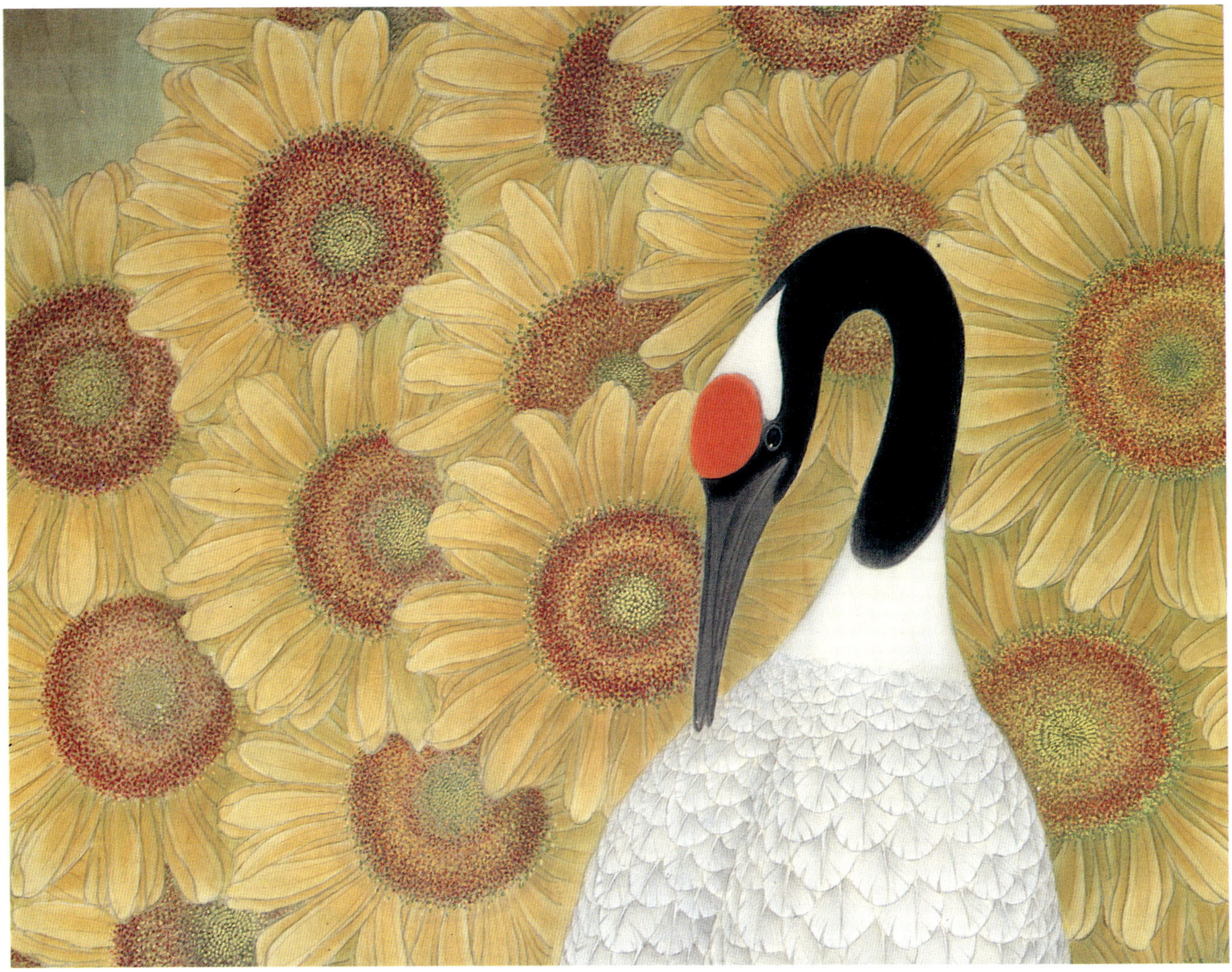

遐寿增年（局部）（1996）　绢本
More Years on Advanced Age
110 × 130cm (1996) on silk (detail)

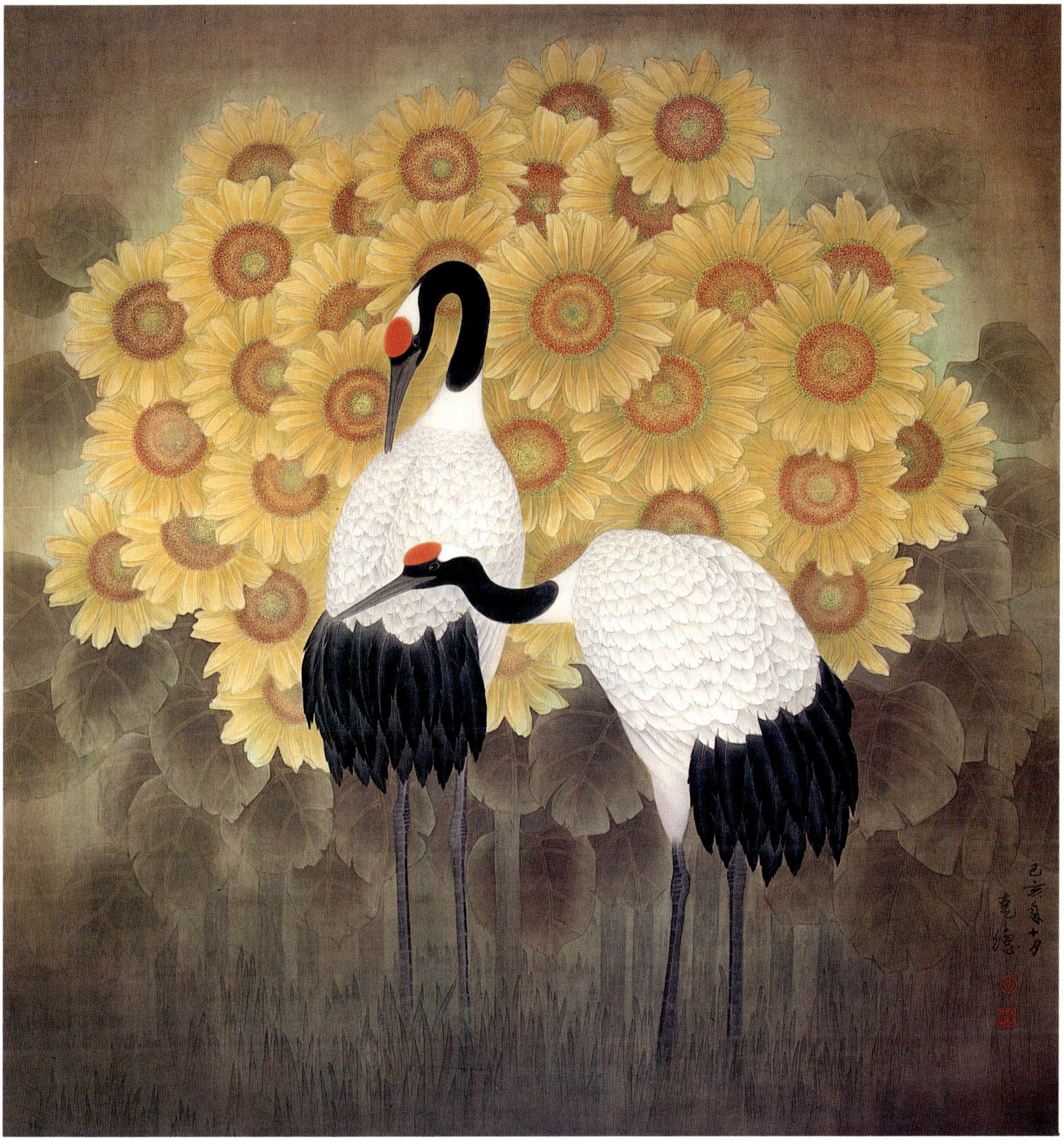

遐寿增年（1996） 绢本
More Years on Advanced Age
110 × 130cm (1996) on silk

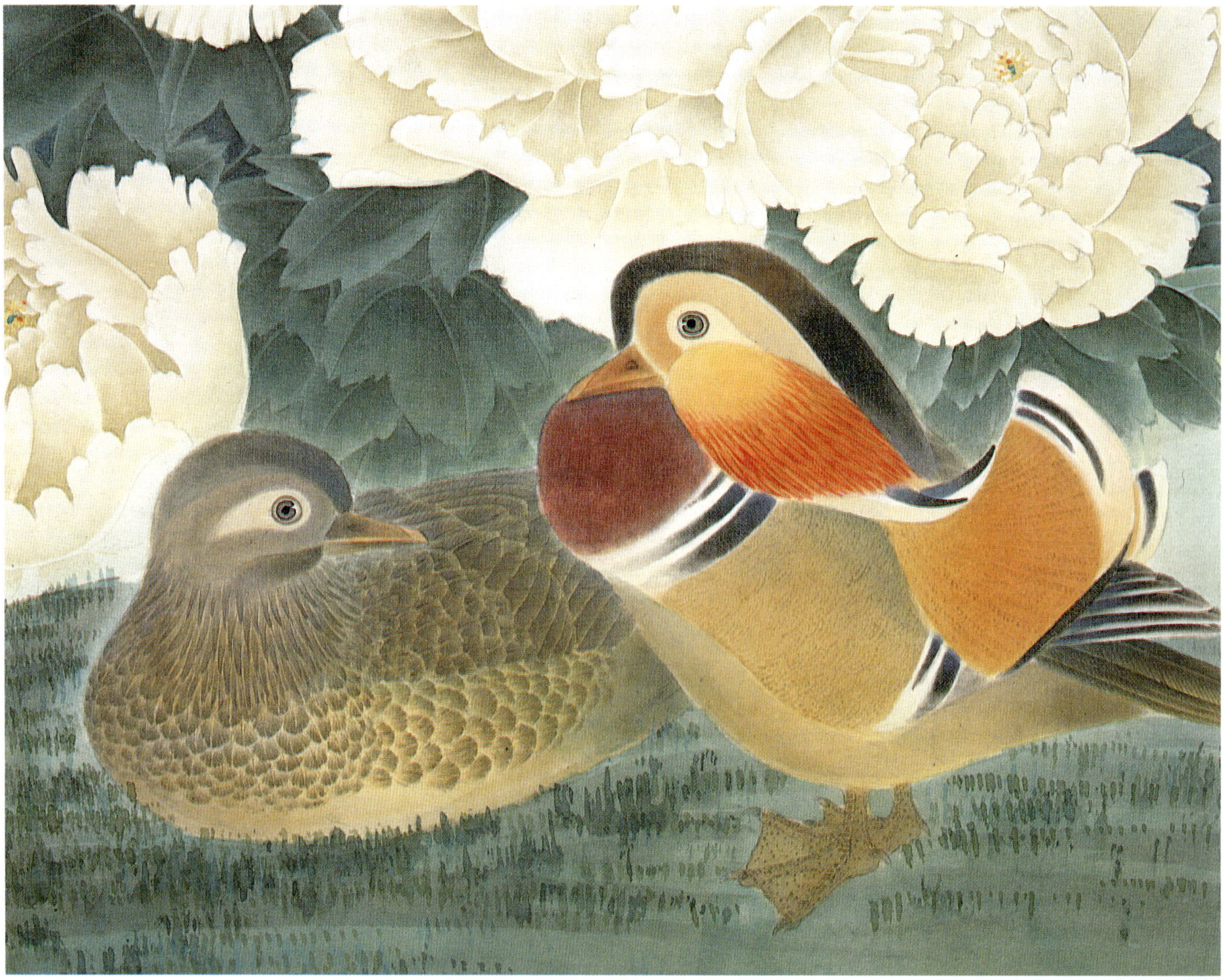

素艳凝情（局部）（1994）　绢本
Flowers and Love
80 × 80cm (1994) on silk (detail)

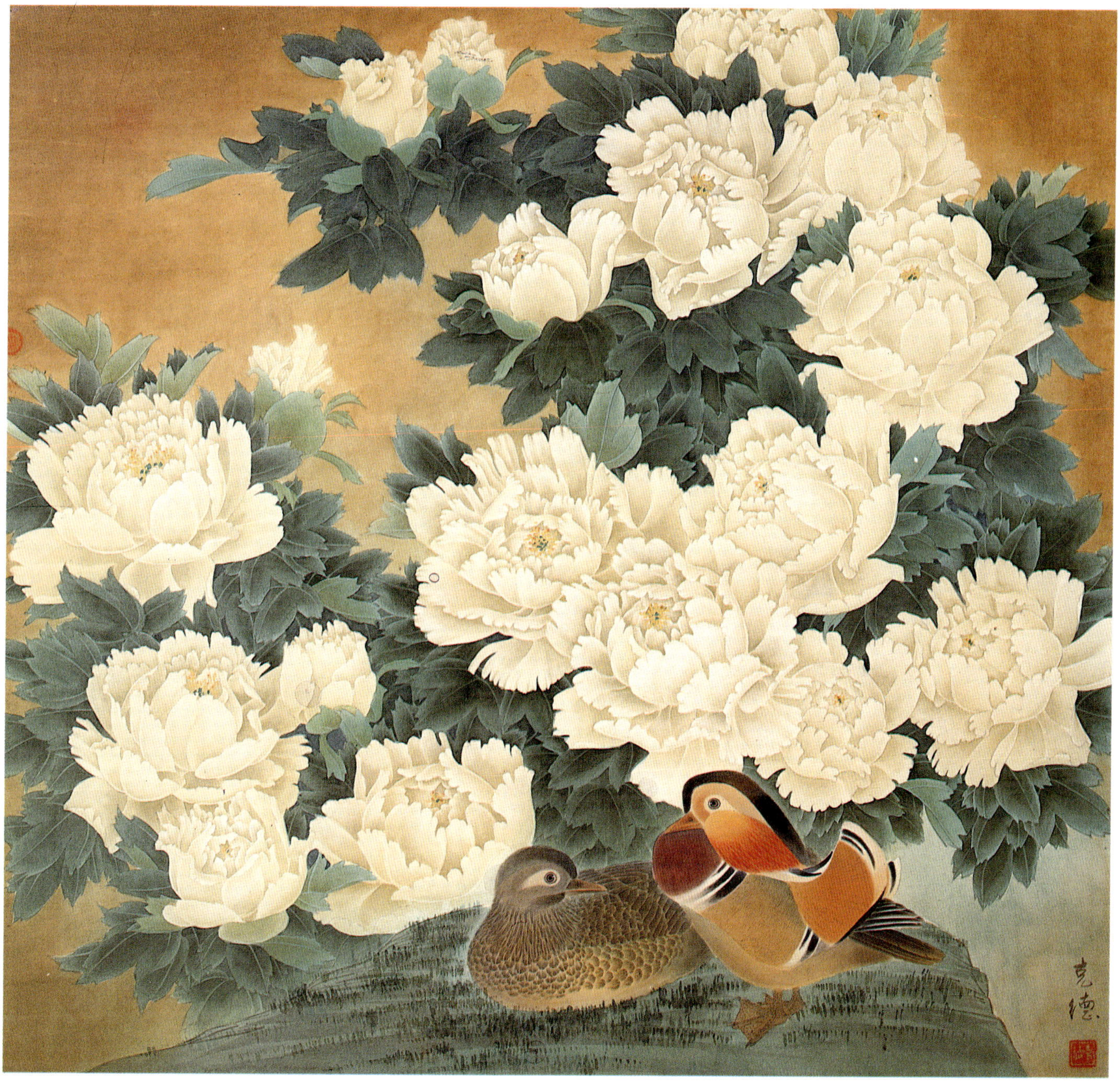

素艳凝情（1994）　绢本
Flowers and Love
80×80cm (1994) on silk

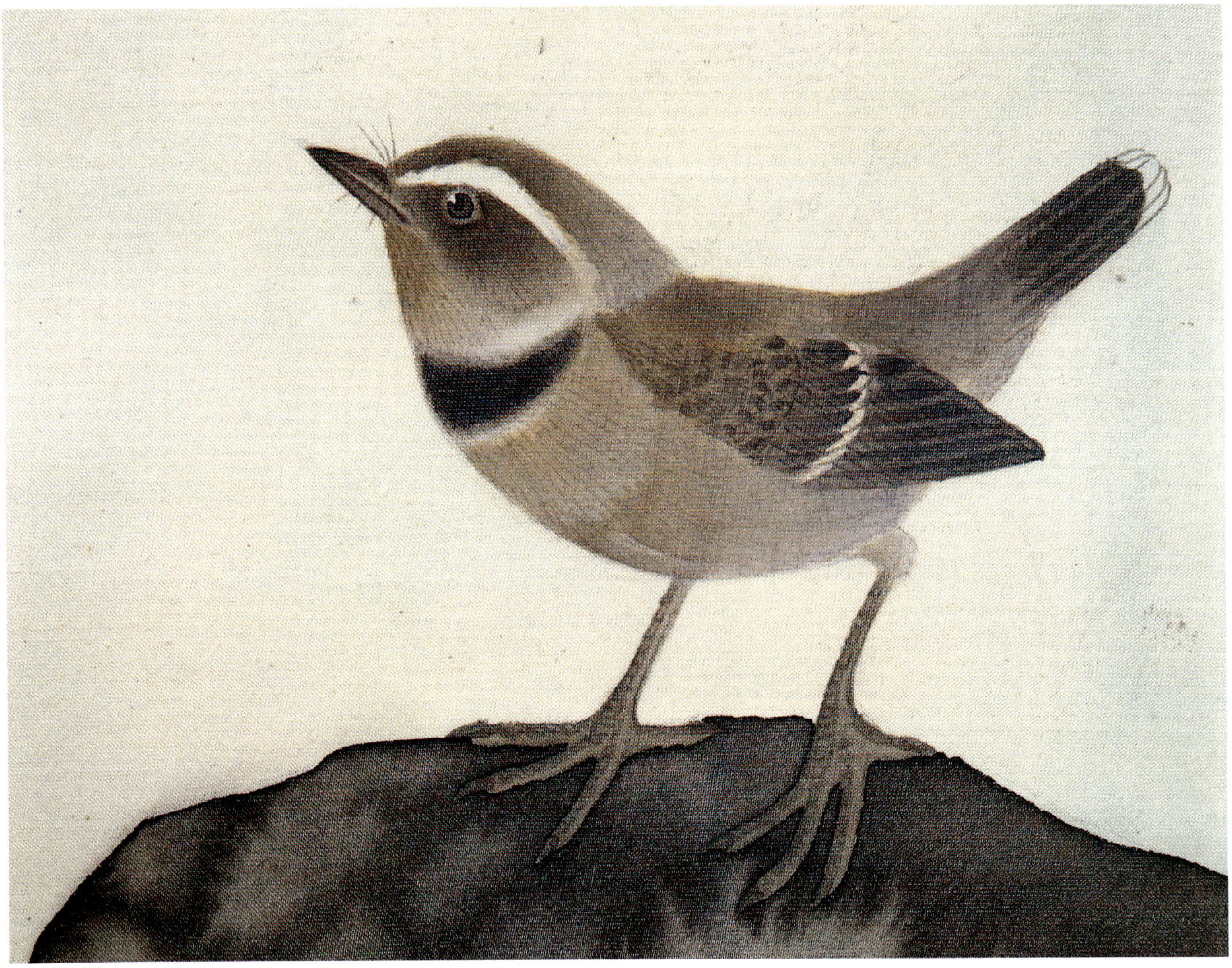

晓风含露（局部）（1996）　绢本
Morning Breeze and Dew
50 × 80cm (1996) on silk (detail)

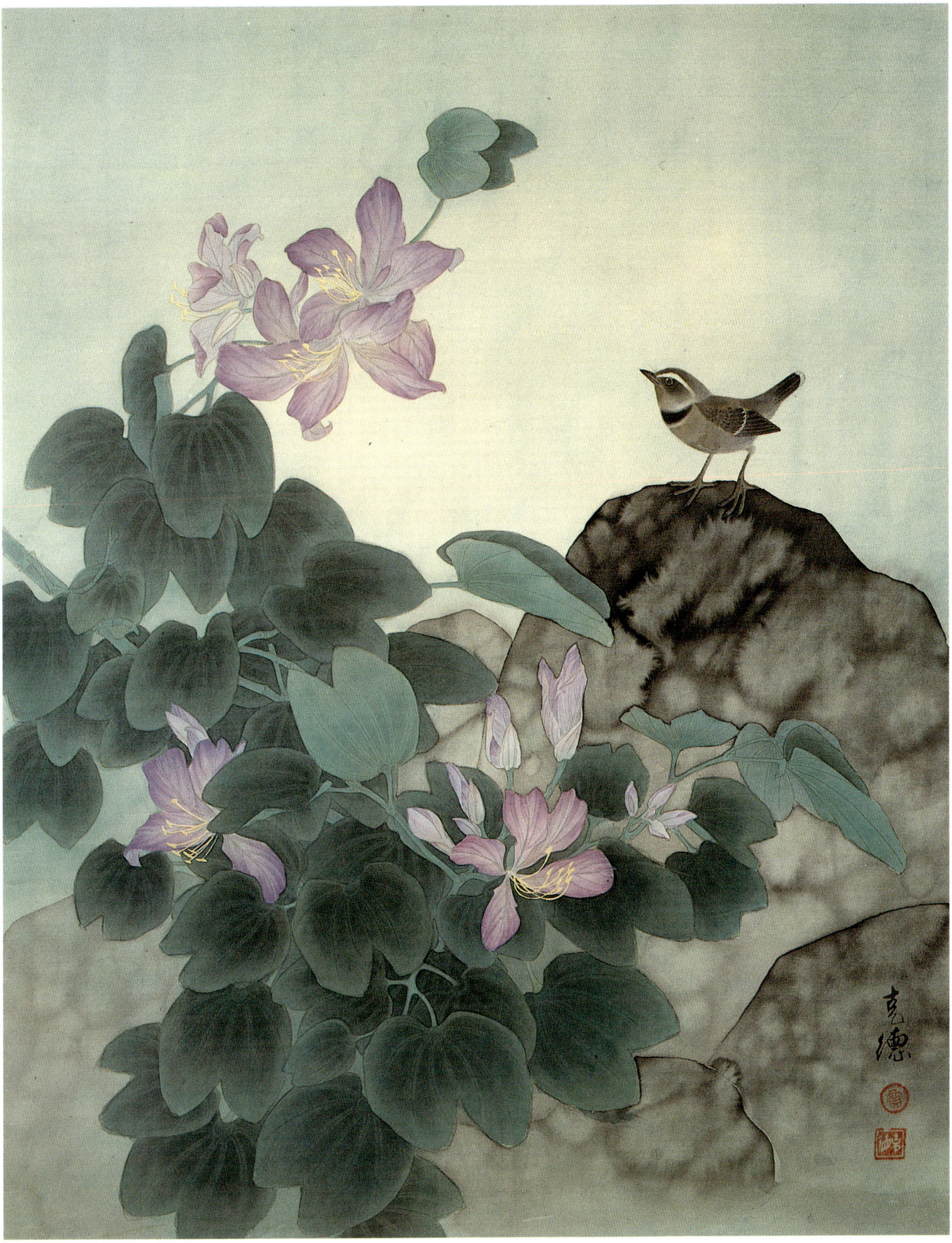

晓风含露（1996） 绢本
Morning Breeze and Dew
50 × 80cm (1996) on silk

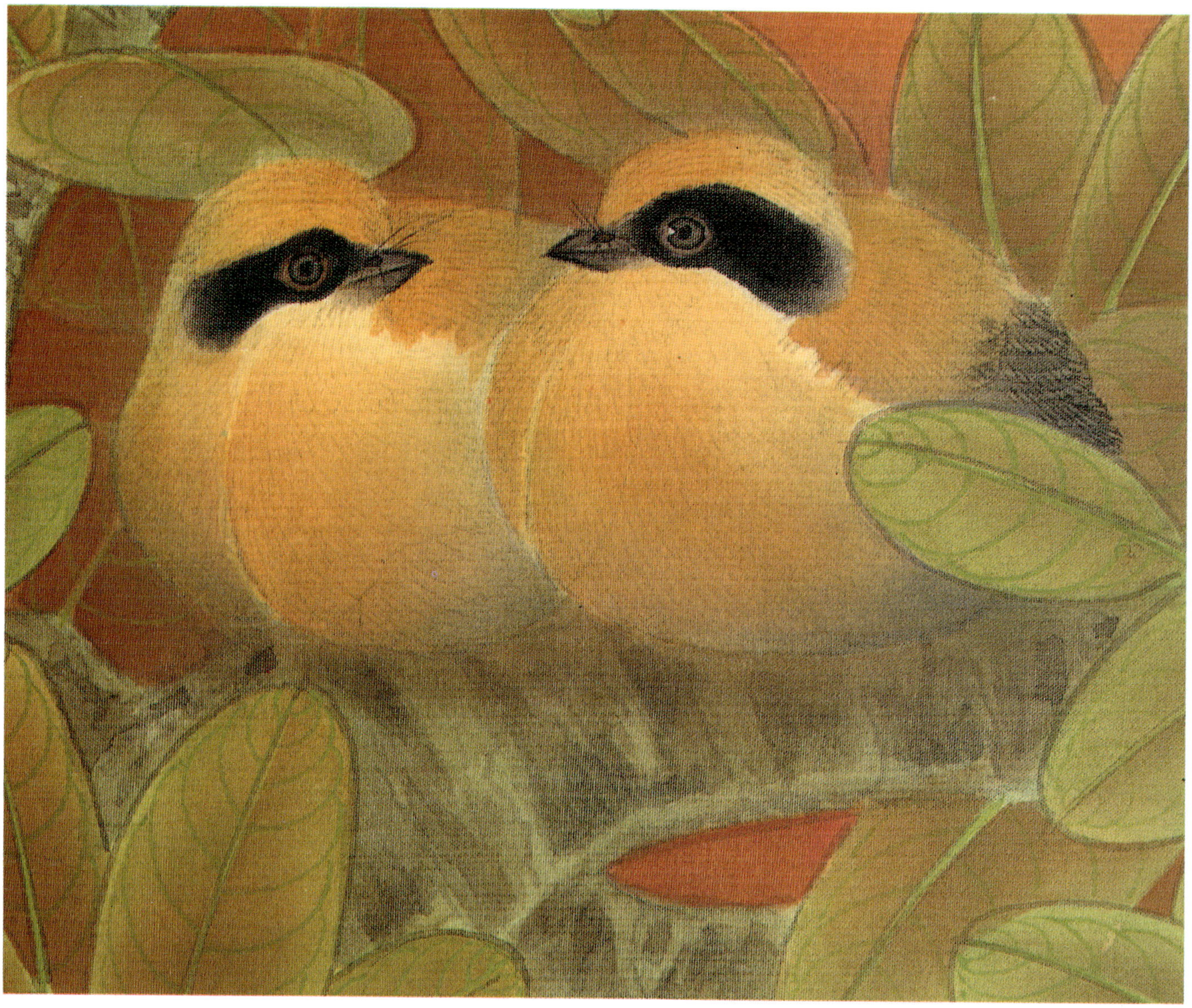

绿润朱光（1996）（局部） 绢本
Green and Crimson
75×85cm (1996) on silk (detail)

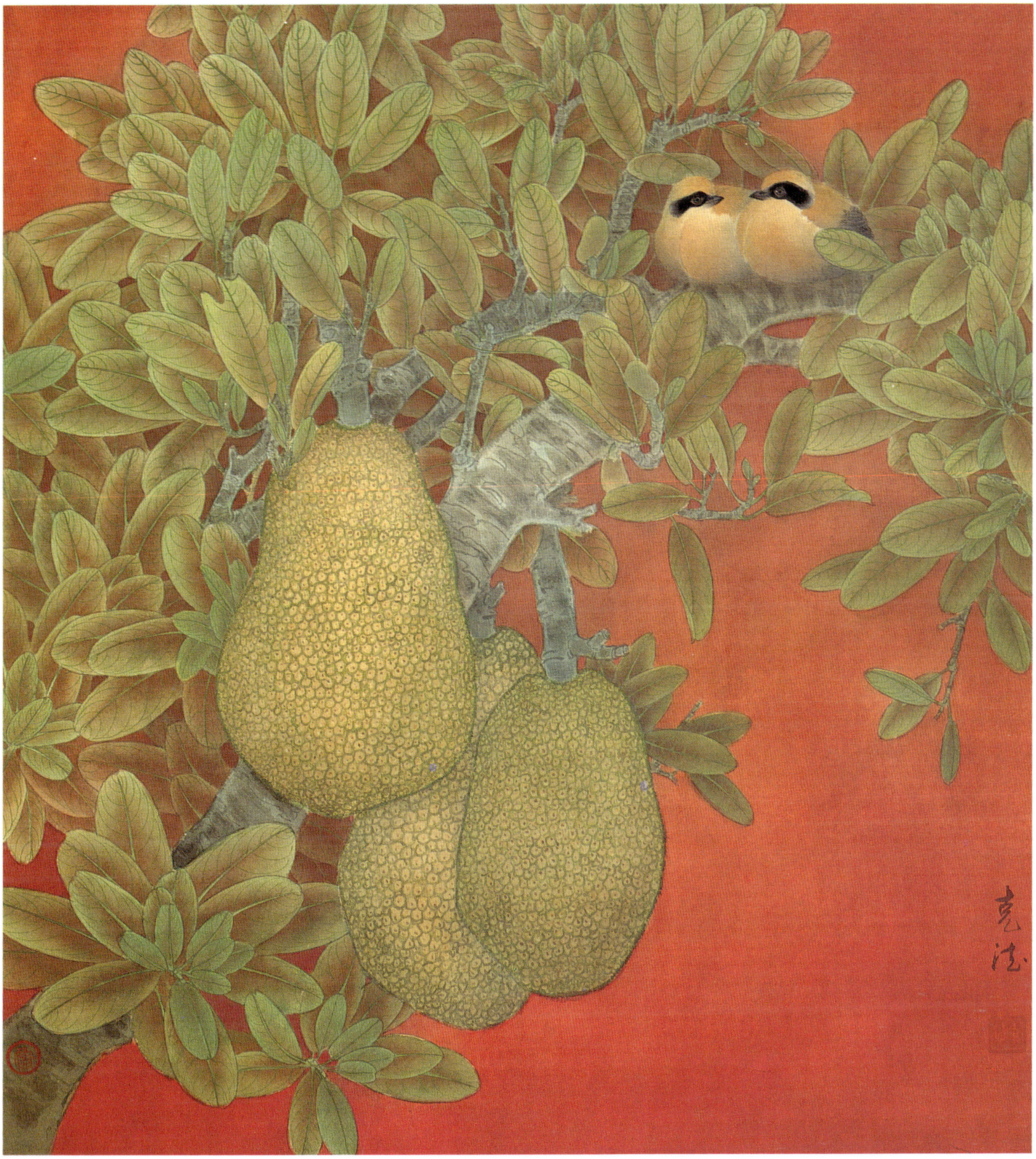

绿润朱光（1996）　绢本
Green and Crimson
75 × 85cm (1996) on silk

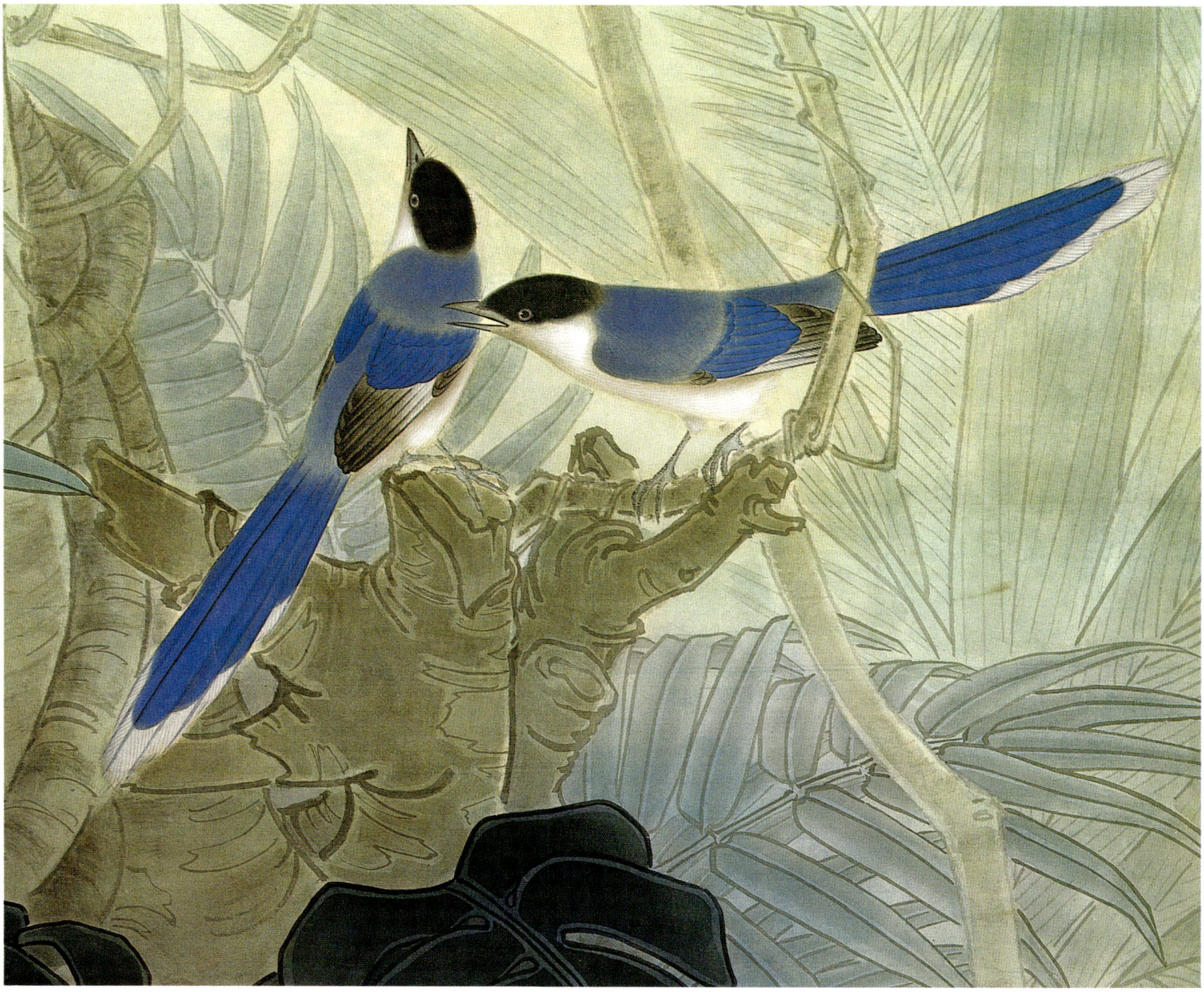

翠羽嬉春（局部）（1985） 绢本
Emerald Feathers Play in Spring
105×110cm (1985) on silk (detail)

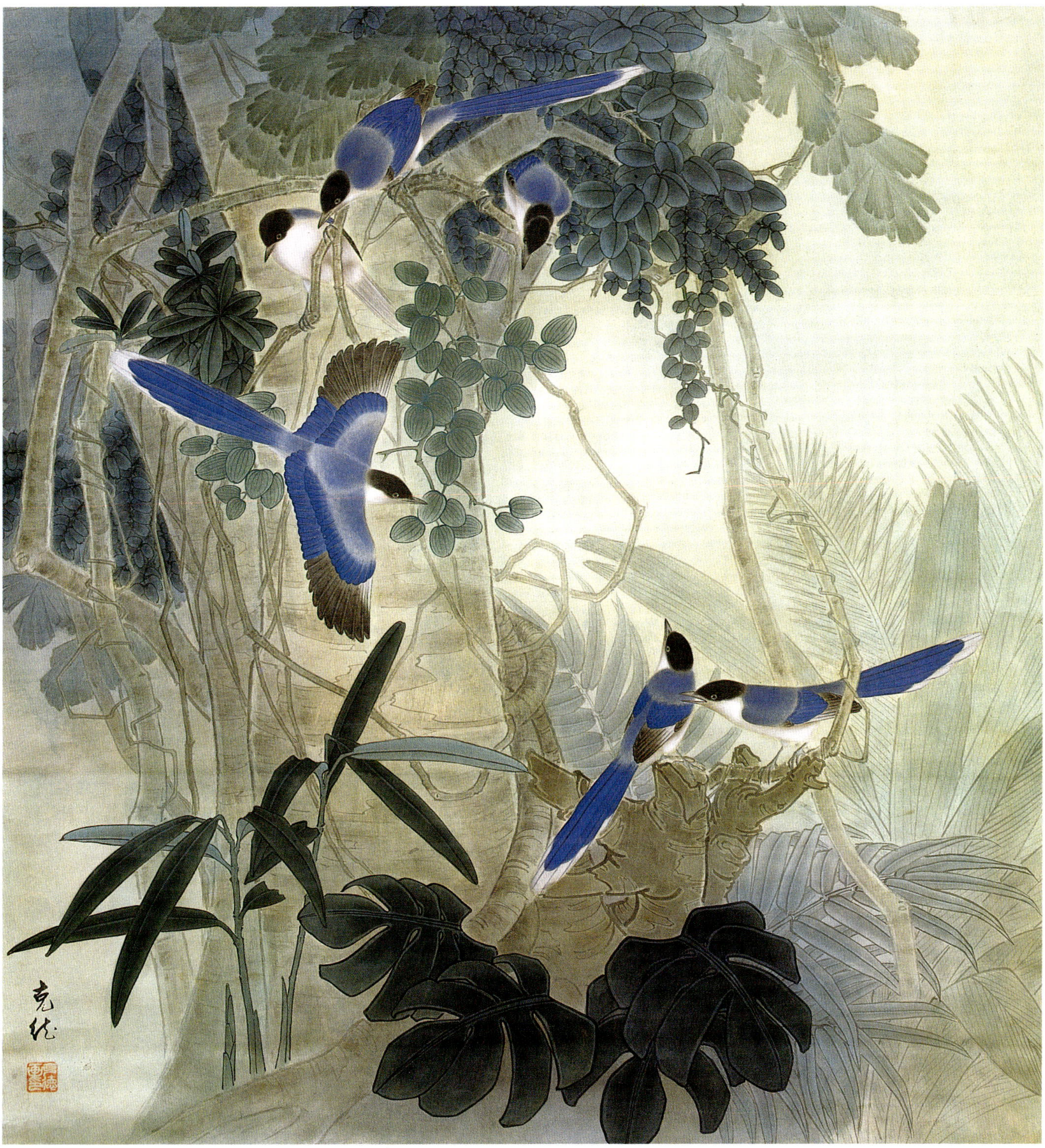

翠羽嬉春（1985） 绢本
Emerald Feathers Play in Spring
105 × 110cm (1985) on silk

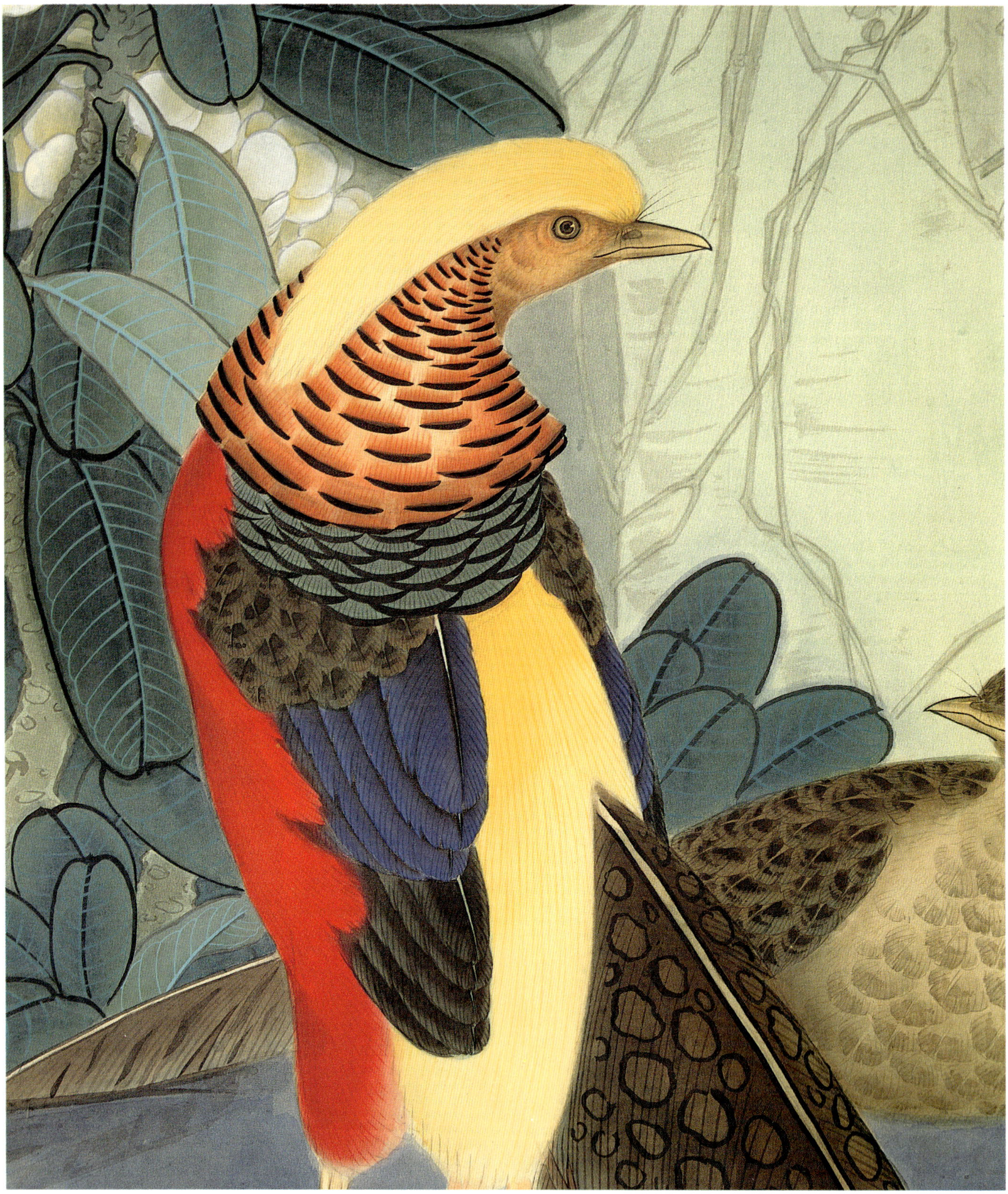

锦羽五德全（局部）（1984） 绢本
Bright Feathers
80 × 120cm (1984) on silk (detail)

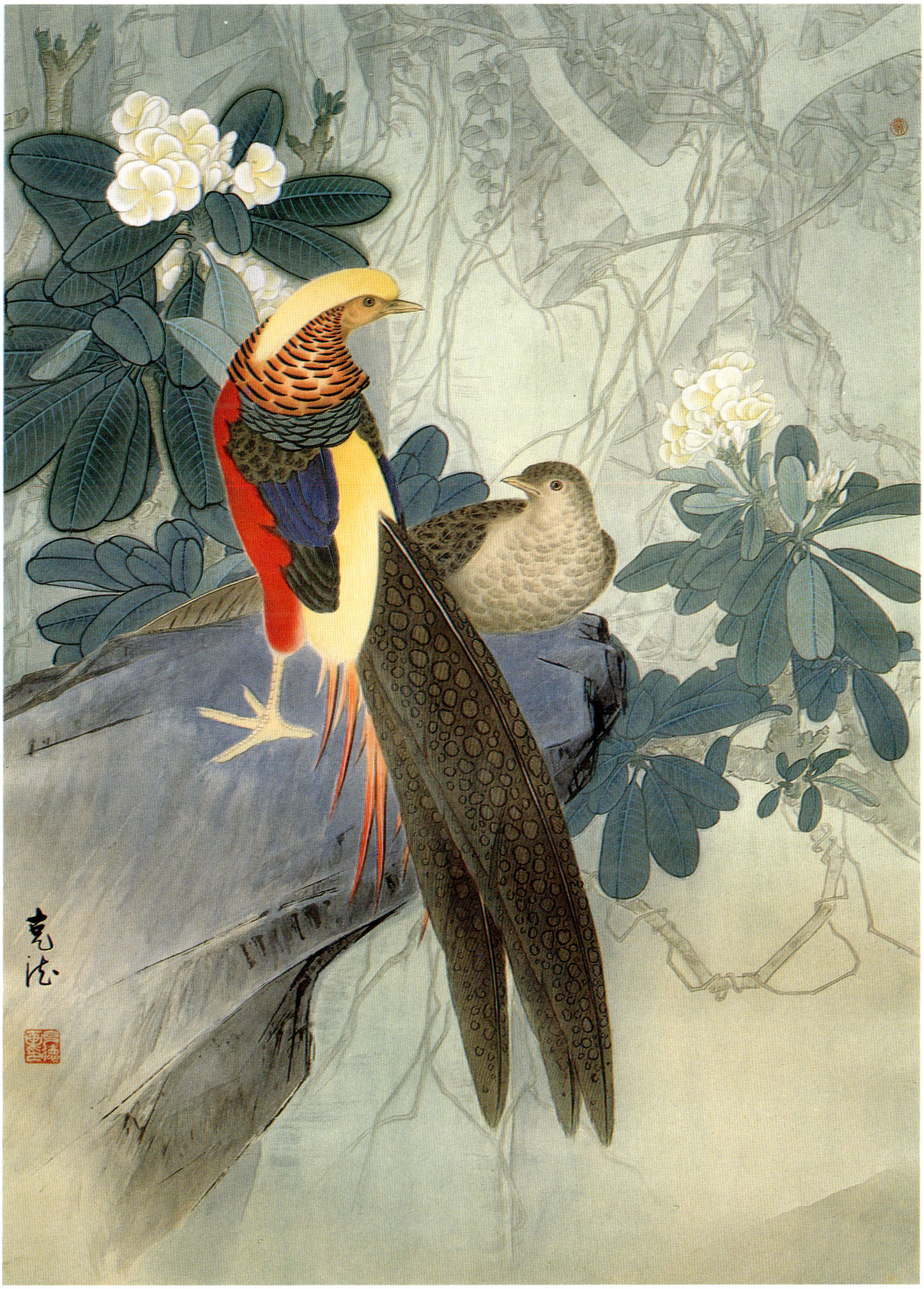

锦羽五德全（1984） 绢本
Bright Feathers
80 × 120cm (1984) on silk

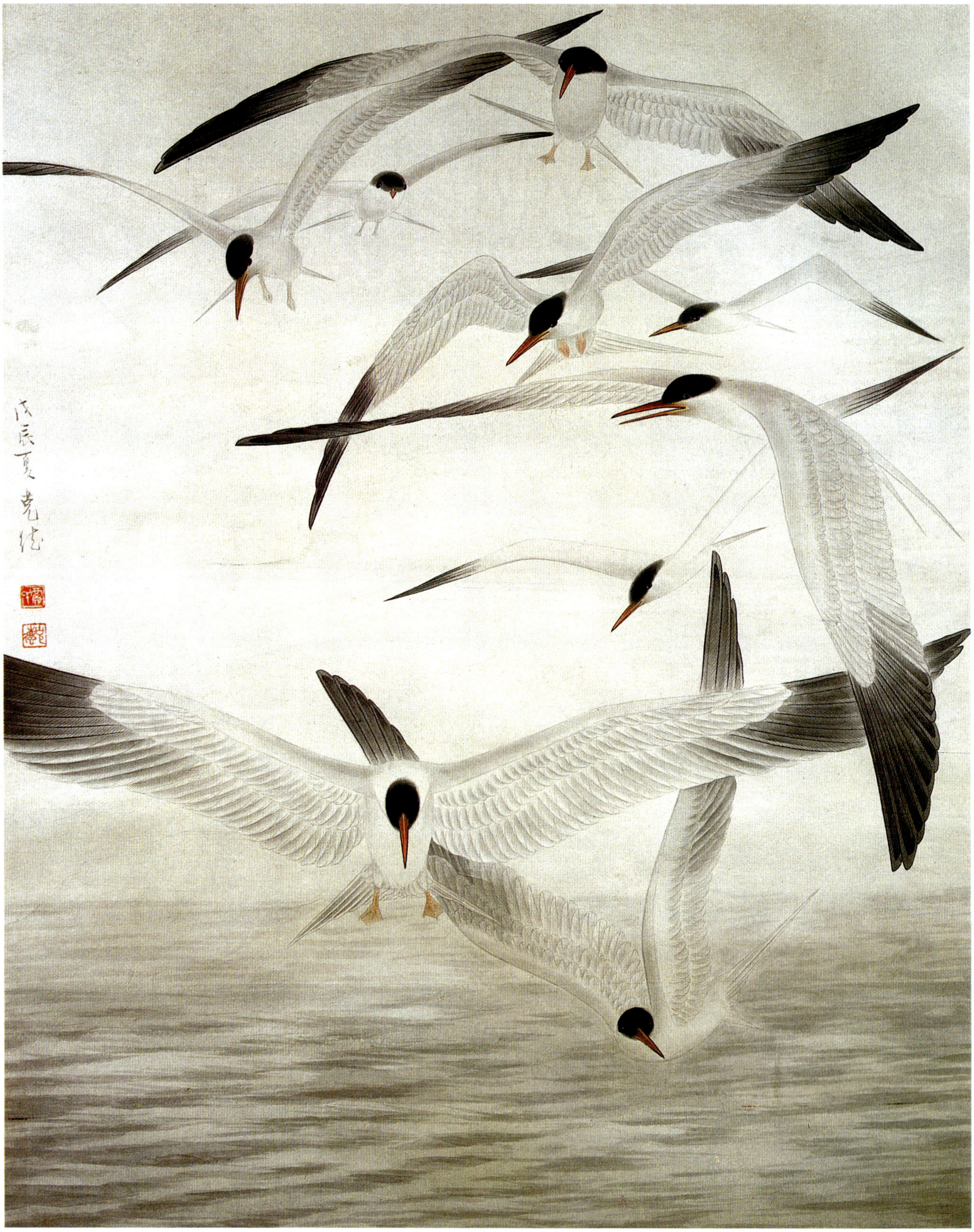

天水一色（1989） 绢本
Sky and Waters of the Same Color
80 × 120cm (1989) on silk

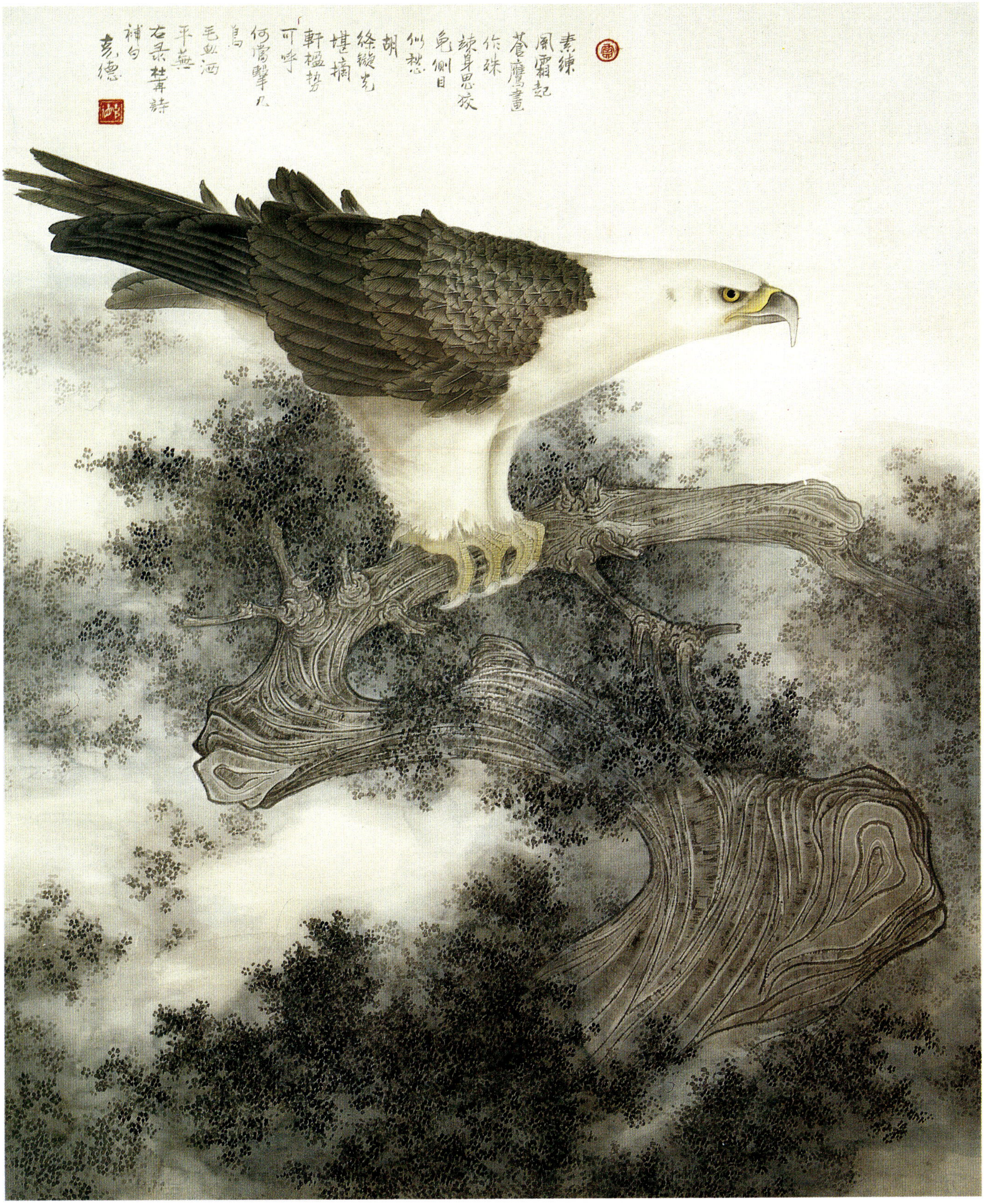

铁翅高旋（1994） 绢本
Steel Wings Up High
80 × 120cm (1994) on silk

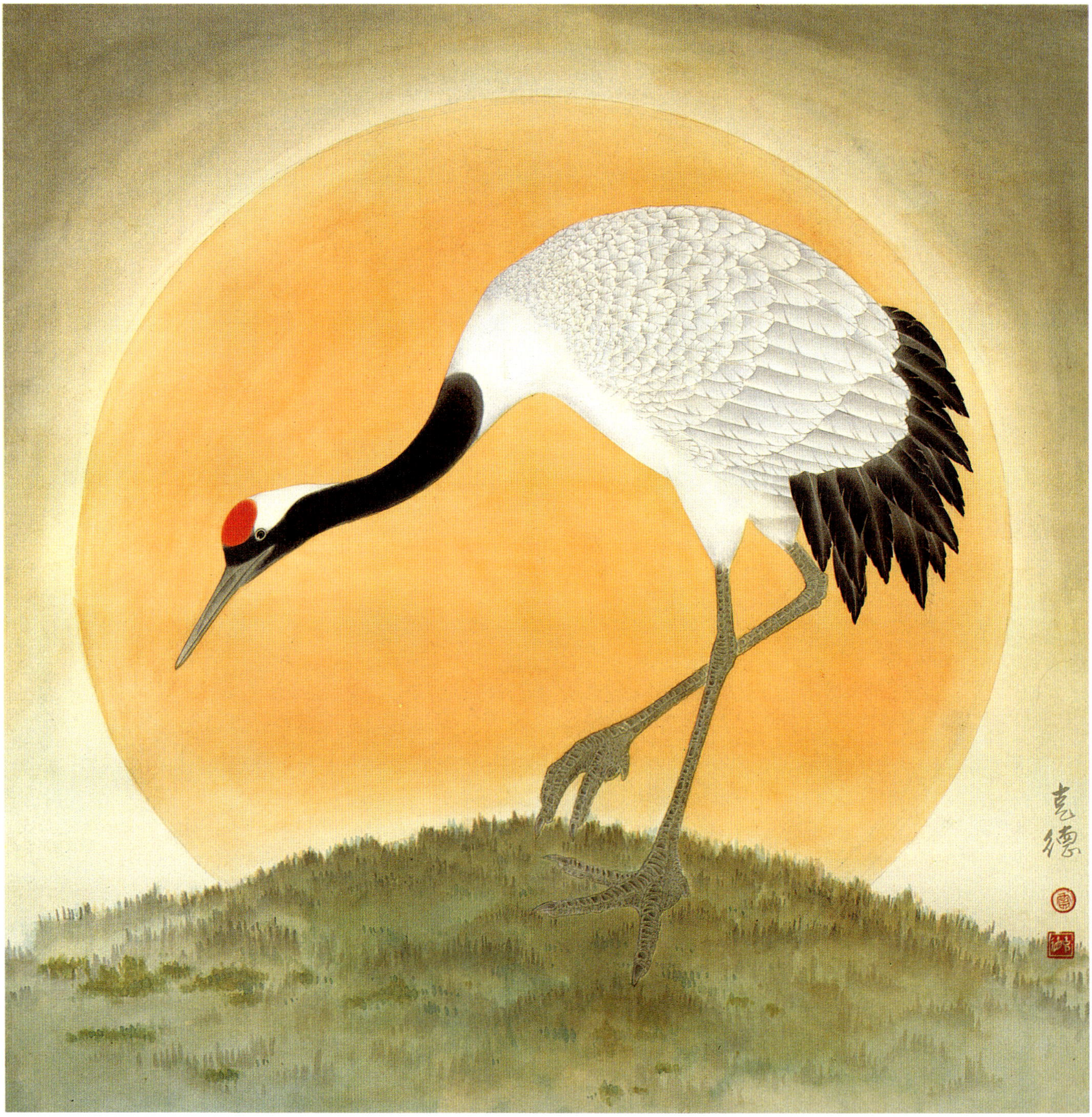

觅——鹤系列之一（1994） 绢本

Searching--One of the Series of Cranes

80 × 80cm (1994) on silk

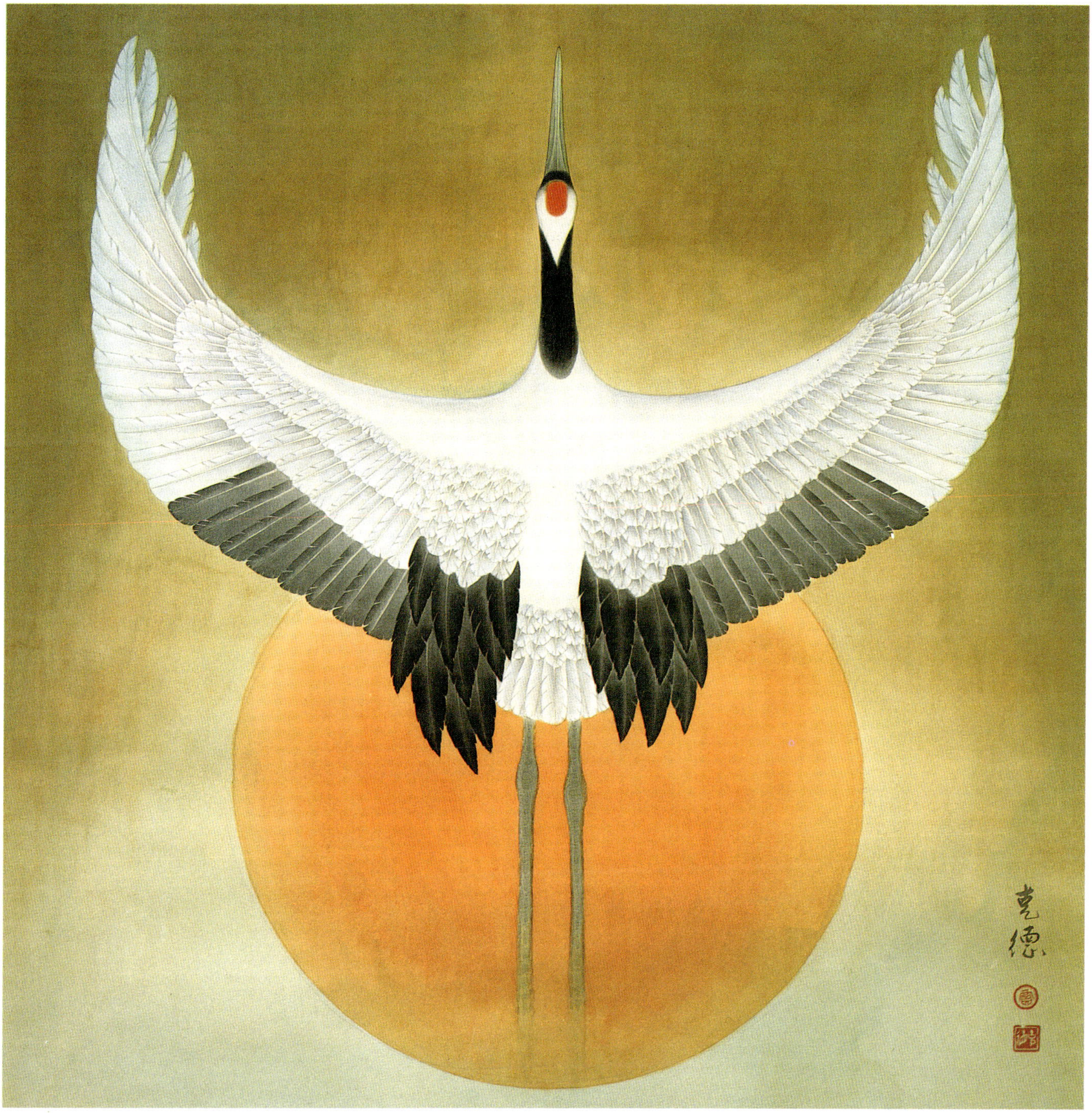

翔——鹤系列之二（1994） 绢本
Flying--One of the Series of Cranes
80×80cm (1994) on silk

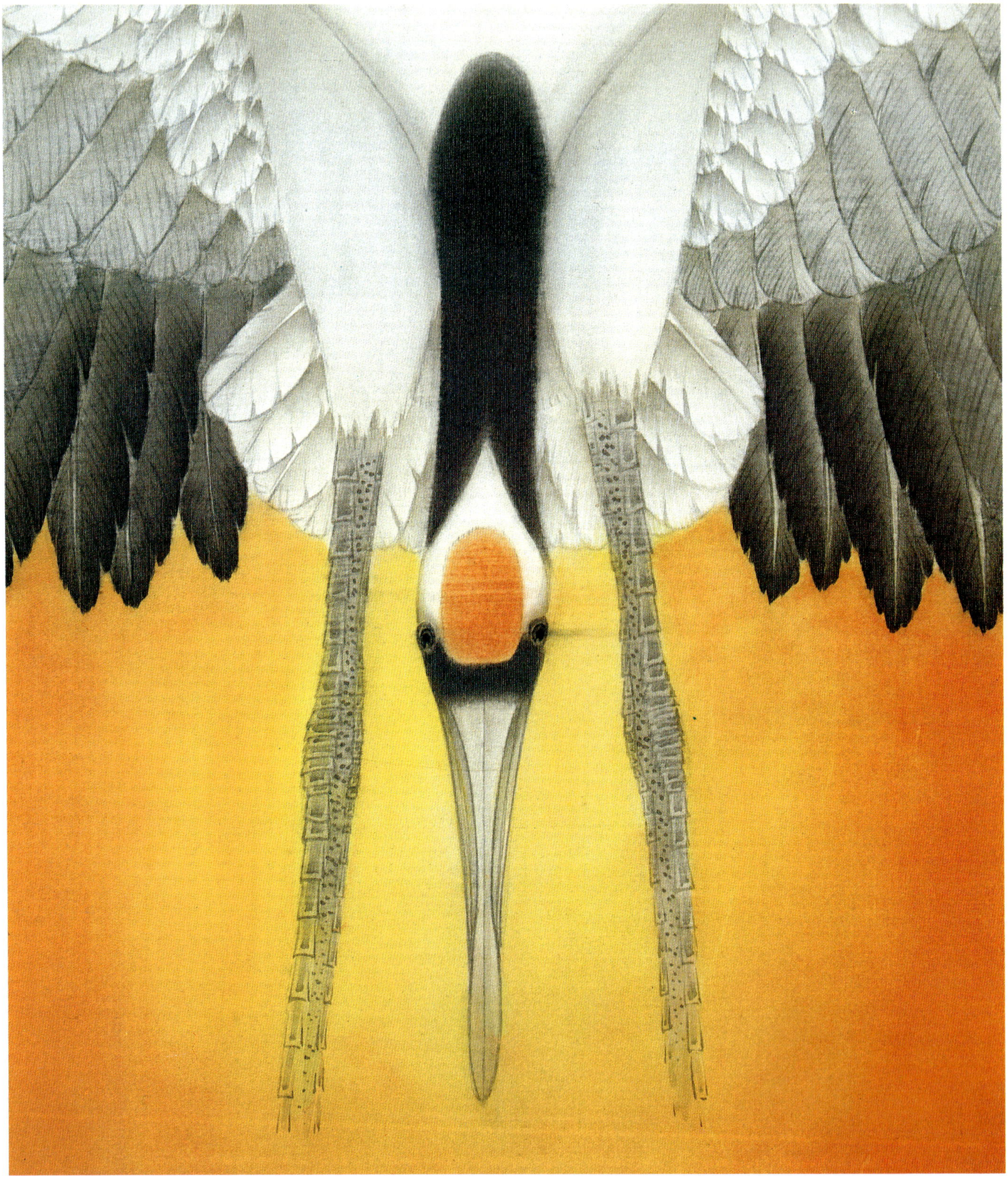

祈——鹤系列之三（局部）（1994） 绢本
Praying--One of the Series of Cranes
80 × 80cm (1994) on silk (detail)

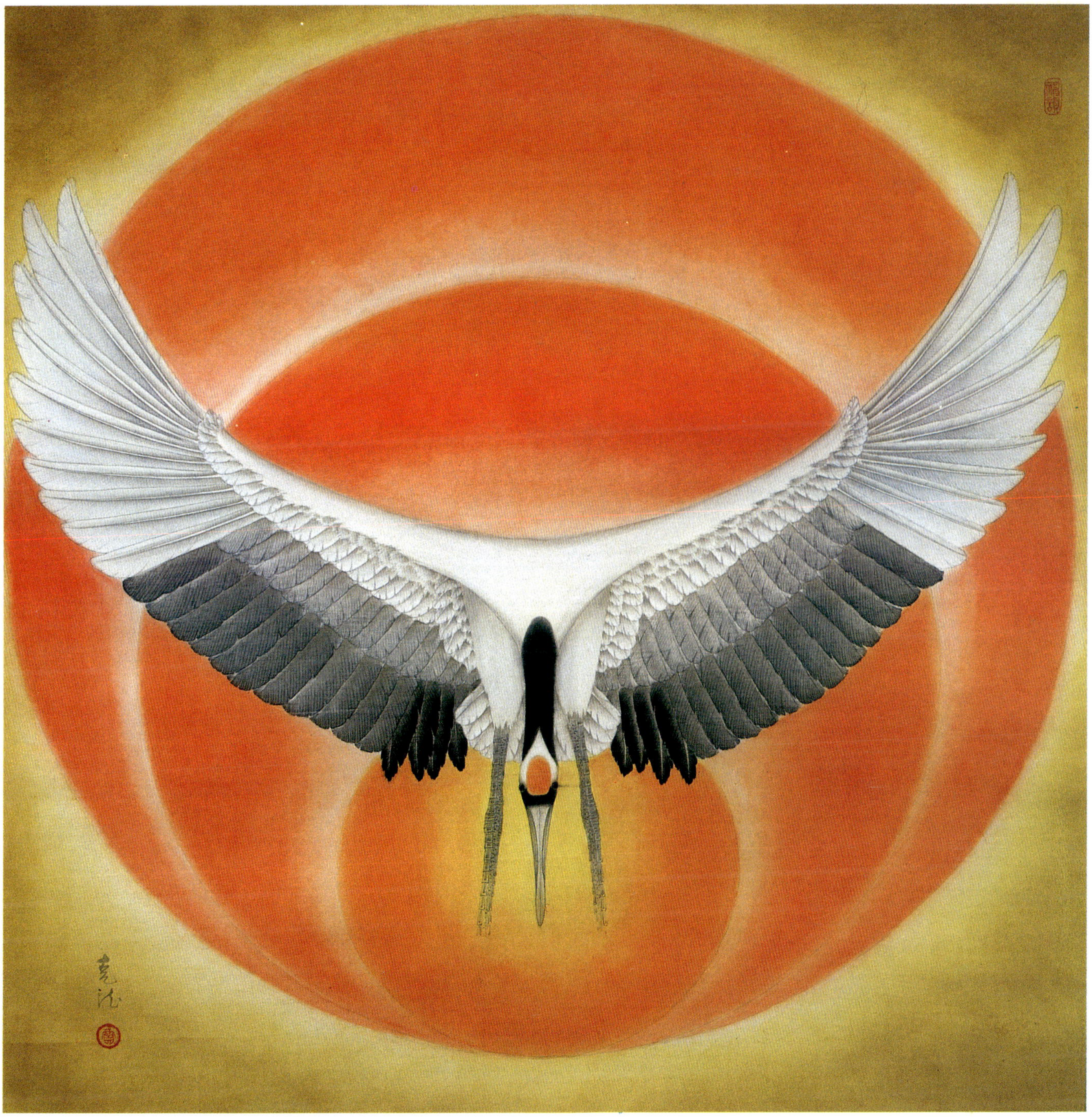

祈——鹤系列之三（1994） 绢本
Praying--One of the Series of Cranes
80 × 80cm (1994) on silk

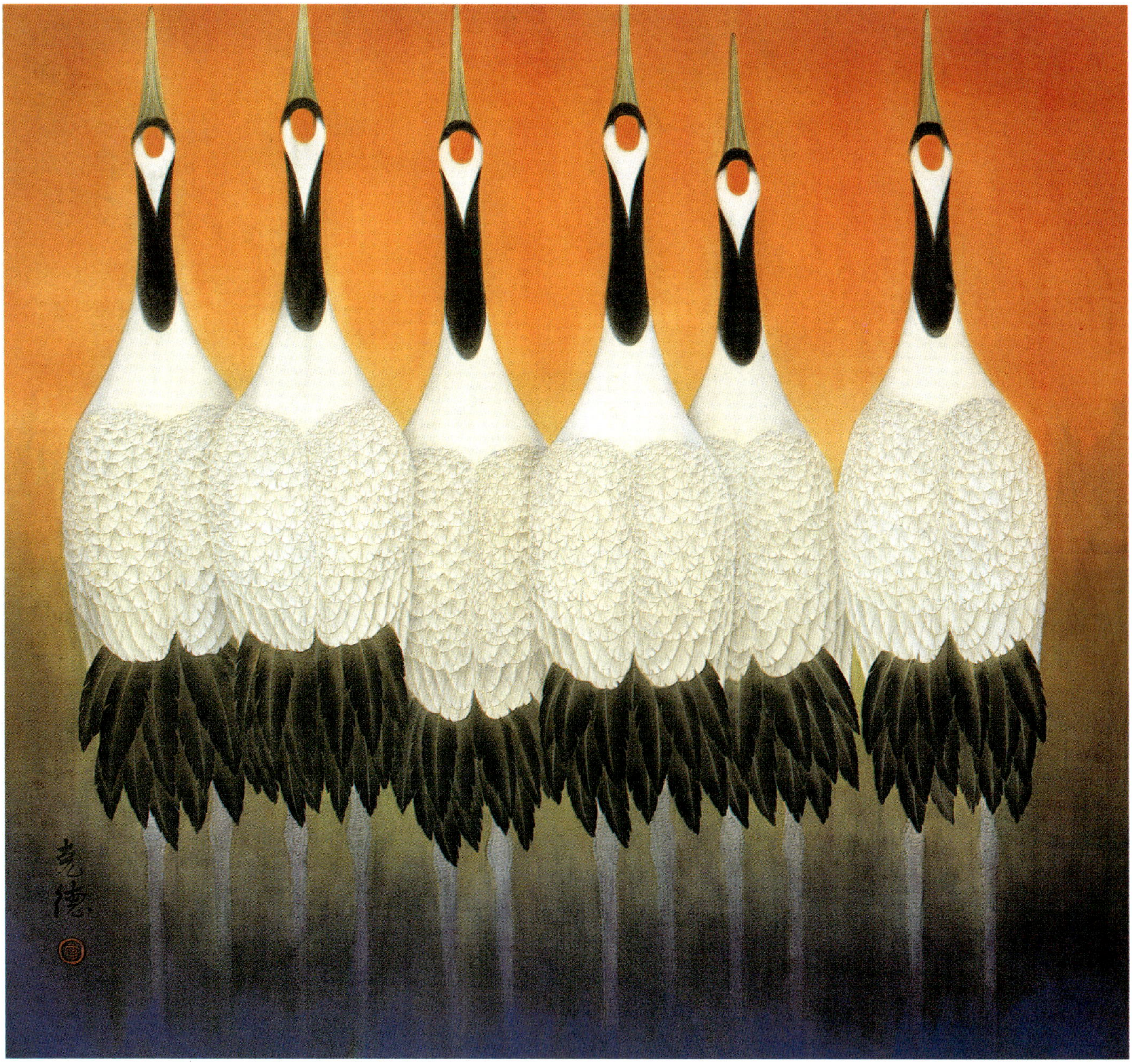

唳——鹤系列之四（1994） 绢本
Crying--One of the Series of Cranes
80 × 80cm (1994) on silk

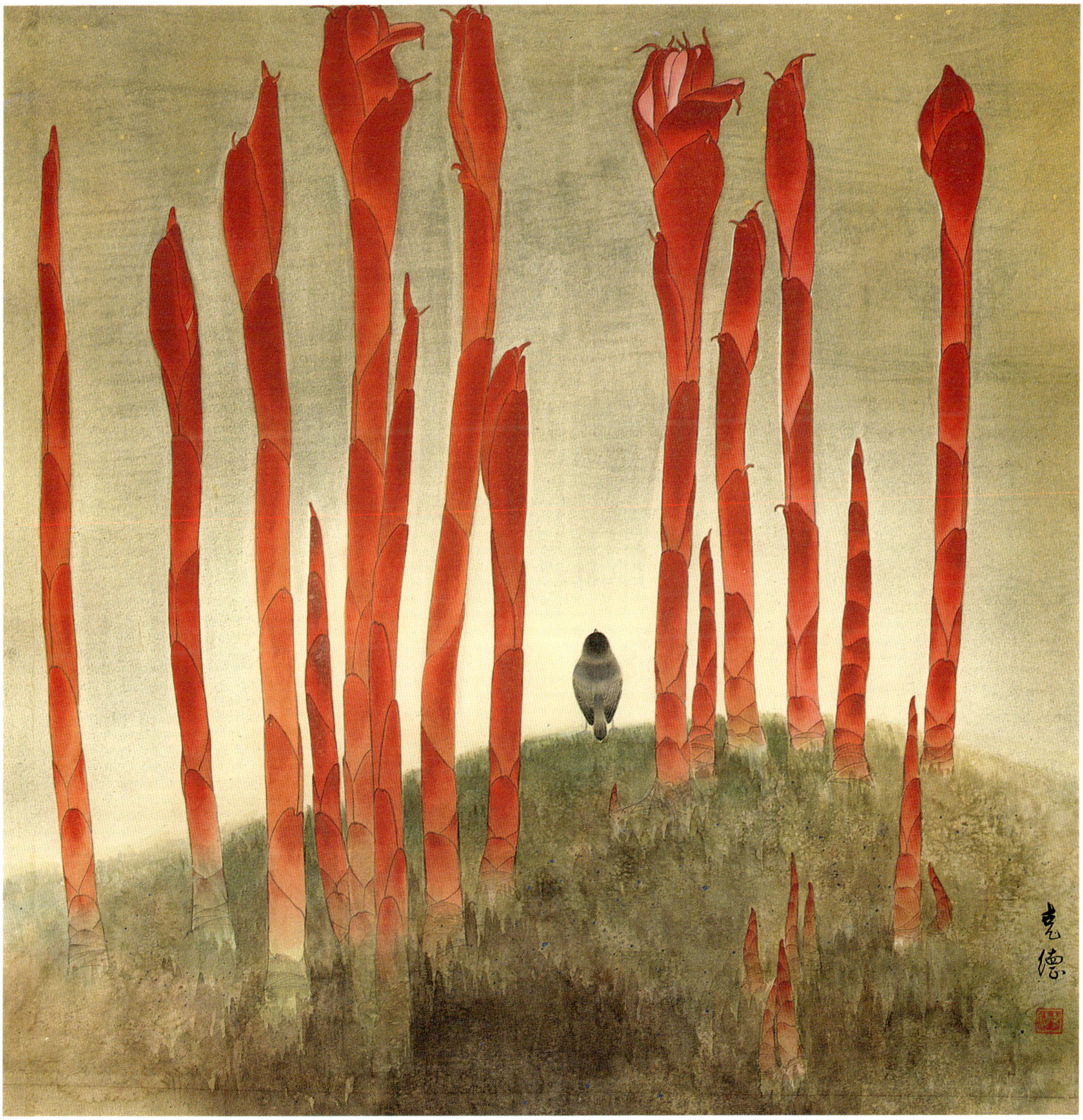

璘柱擎天（1989） 绢本
Pillars Reaching to the Sky
75 × 75cm (1989) on silk

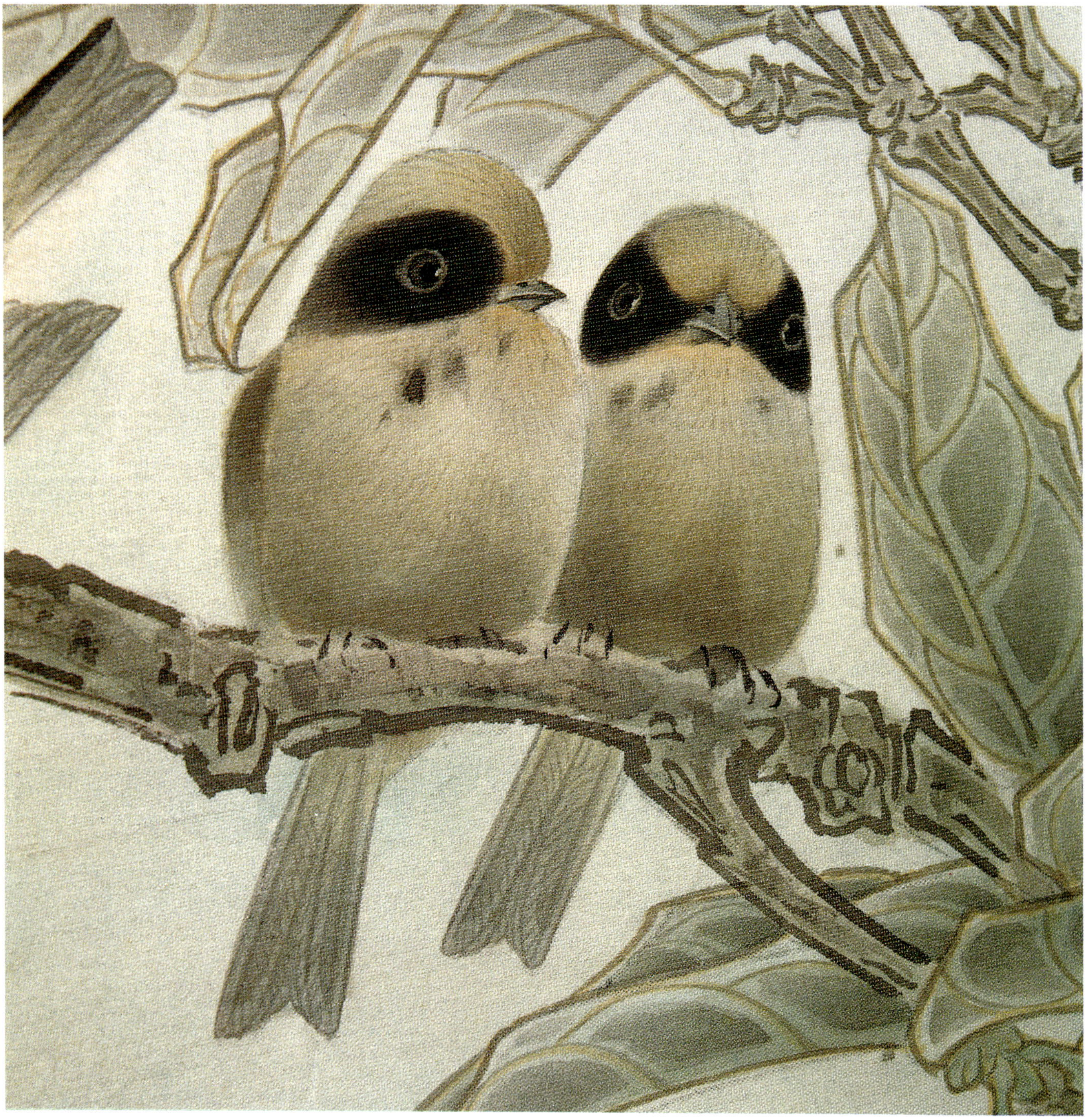

文鸟媚春（局部）（1995） 绢本
Mannikins in Spring
45 × 75cm (1995) on silk (detail)

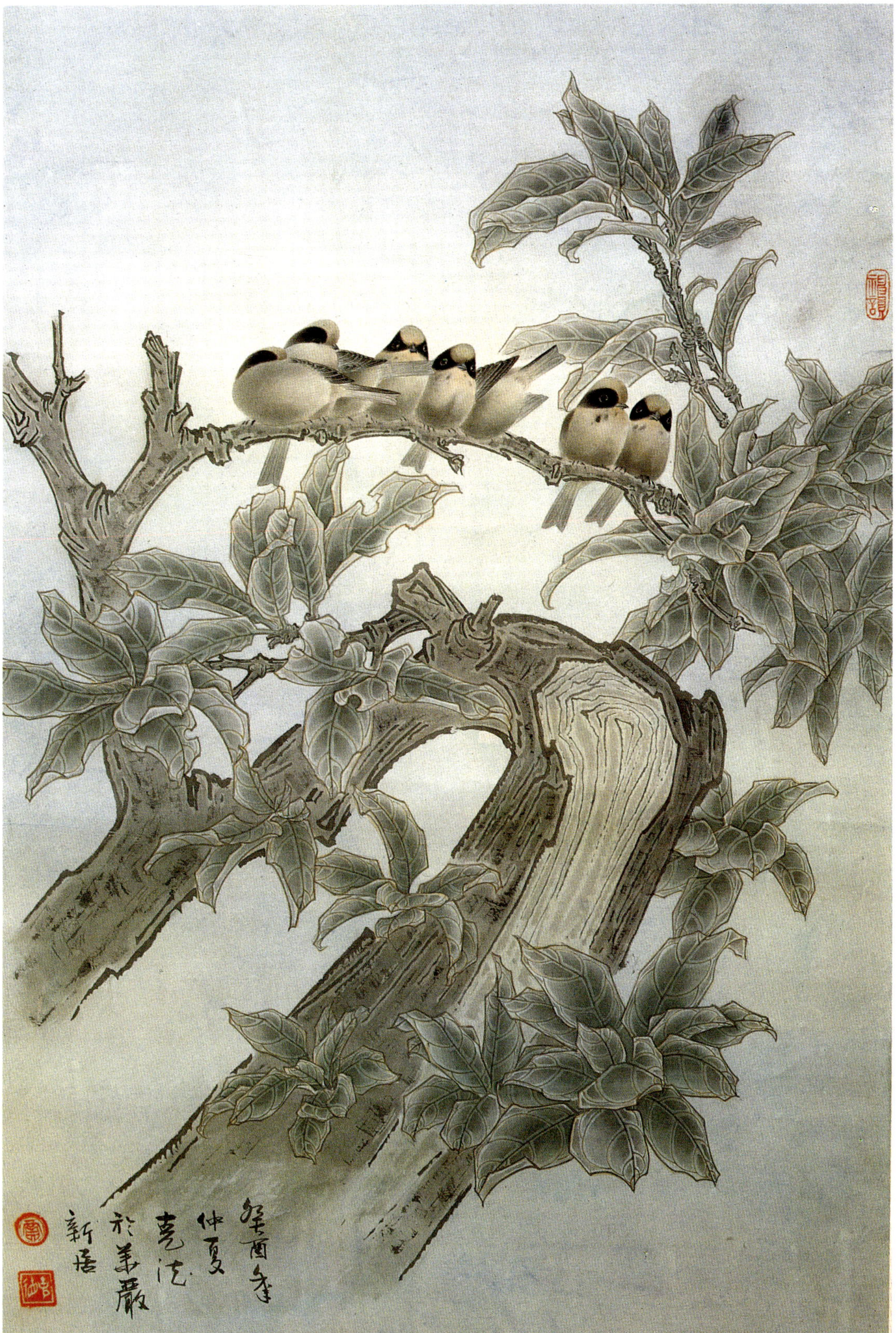

文鸟媚春（1995） 绢本
Mannikins in Spring
45 × 75cm (1995) on silk

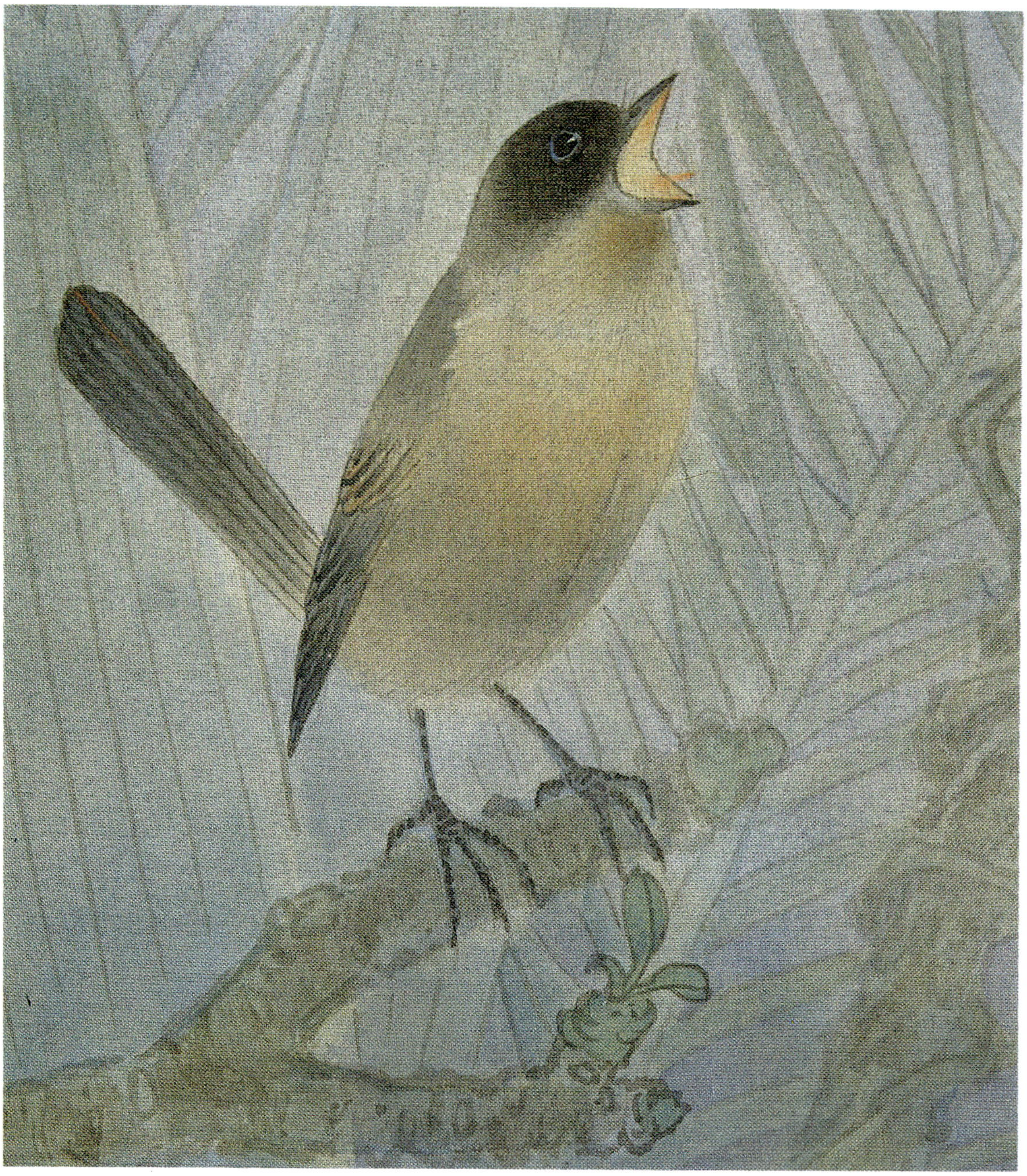

雨林晨歌（局部）（1986） 绢本
Morning Song in Trees After Rain
45 × 80cm (1986) on silk (detail)

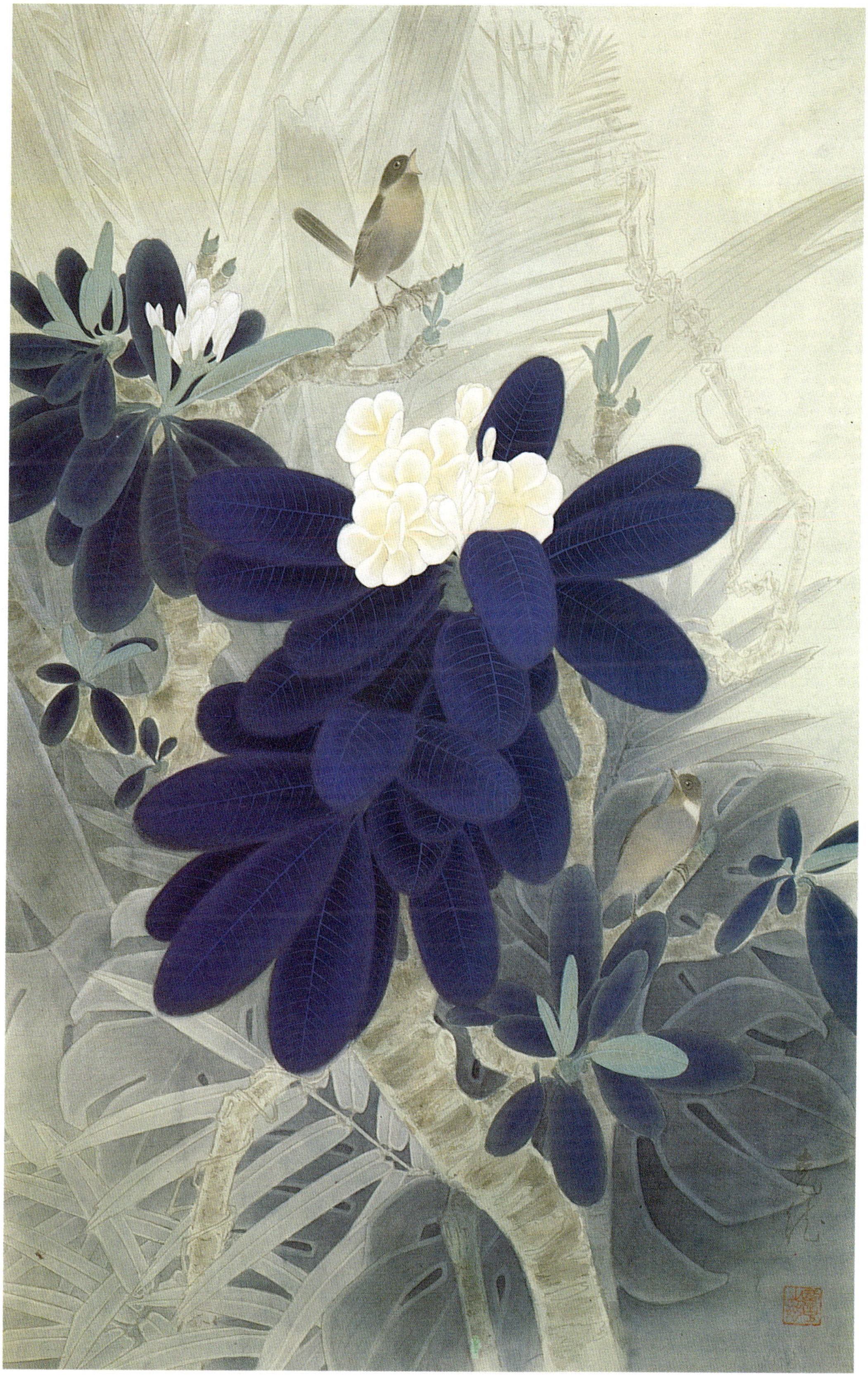

雨林晨歌（1986） 绢本
Morning Song in Trees After Rain
45 × 80cm (1986) on silk

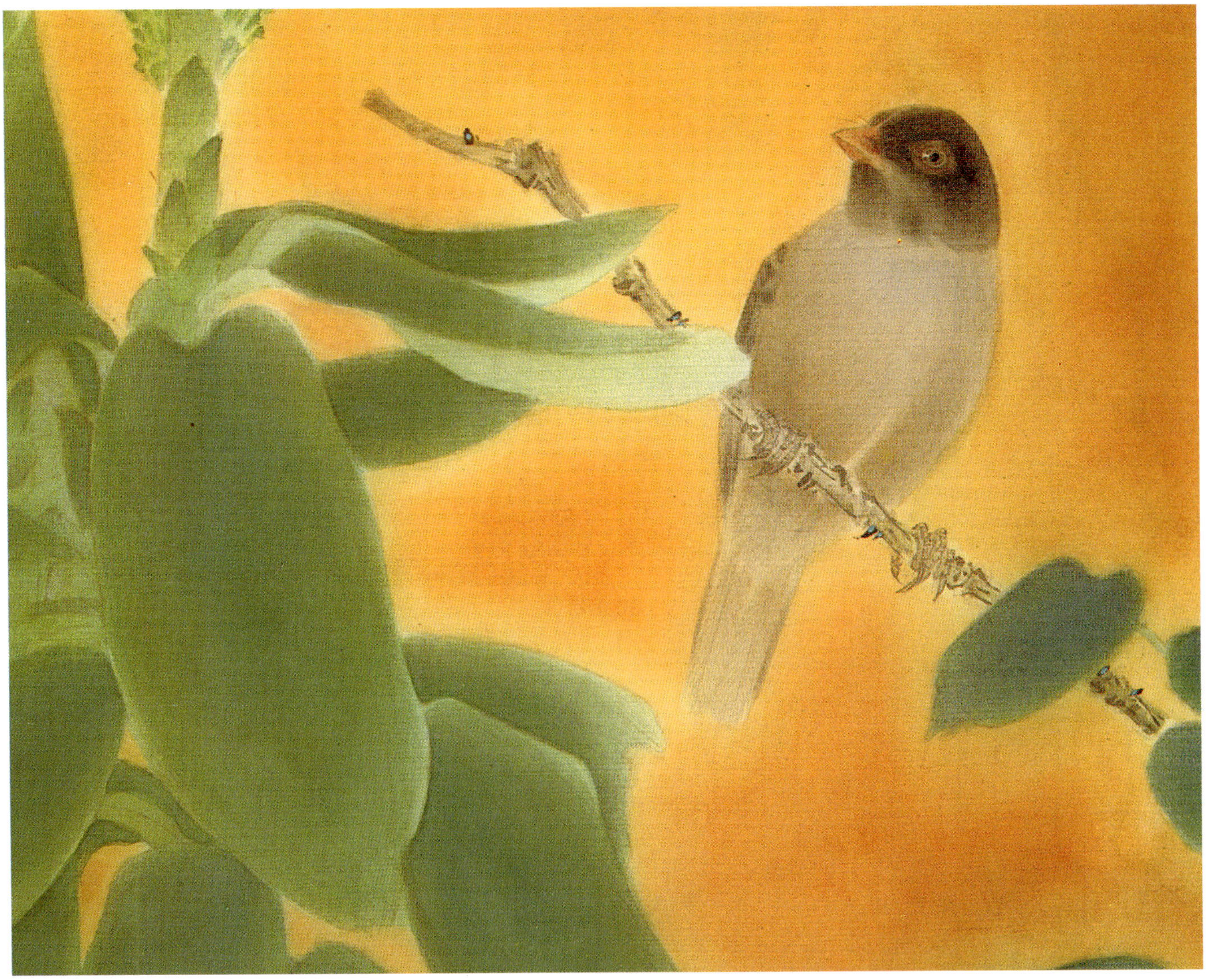

春日晴和（局部）（1997） 绢本
A Clear Spring Day
50 × 80cm (1997) on silk (detail)

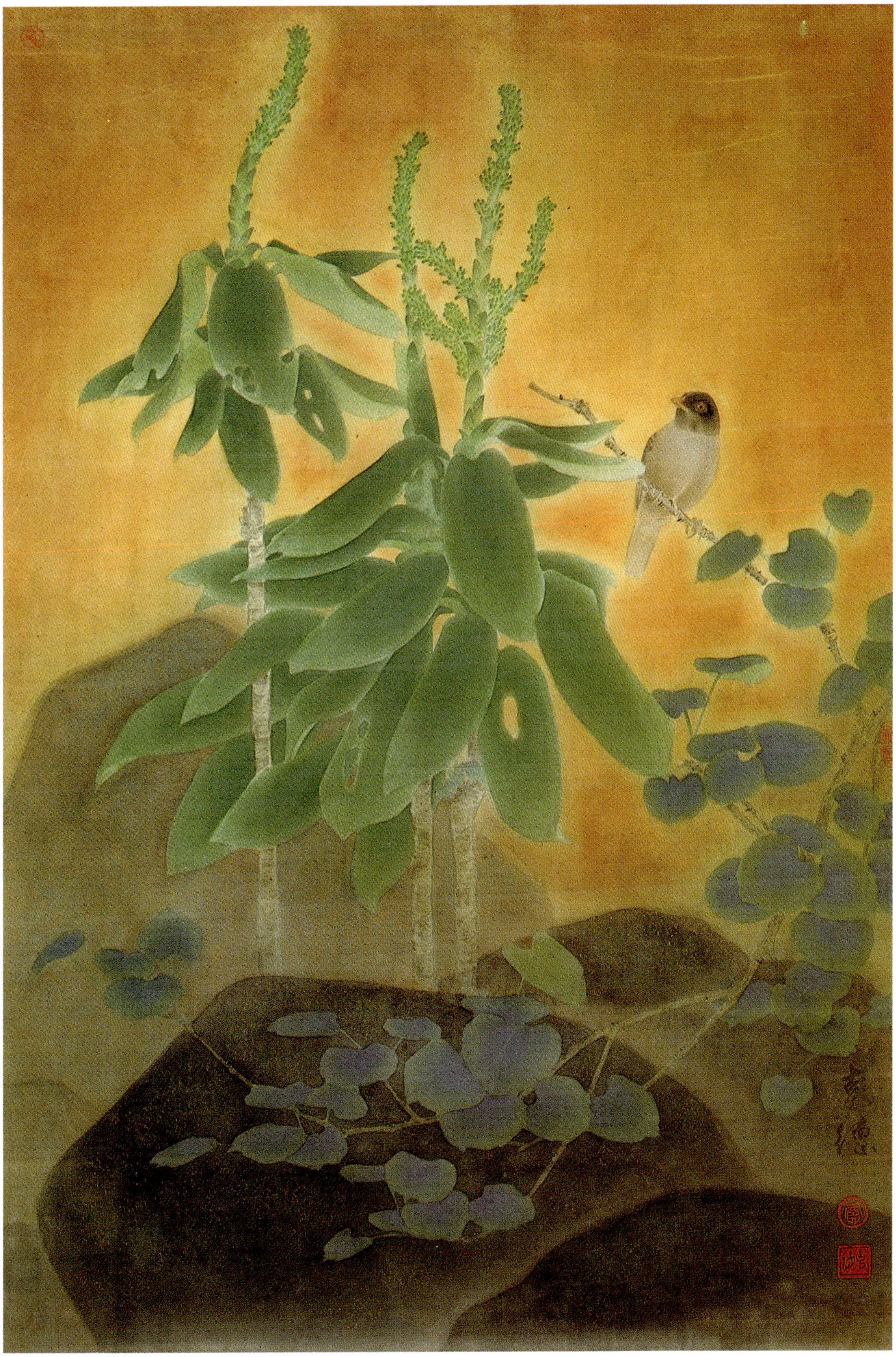

春日晴和（1997） 绢本
A Clear Spring Day
50 × 80cm (1997) on silk

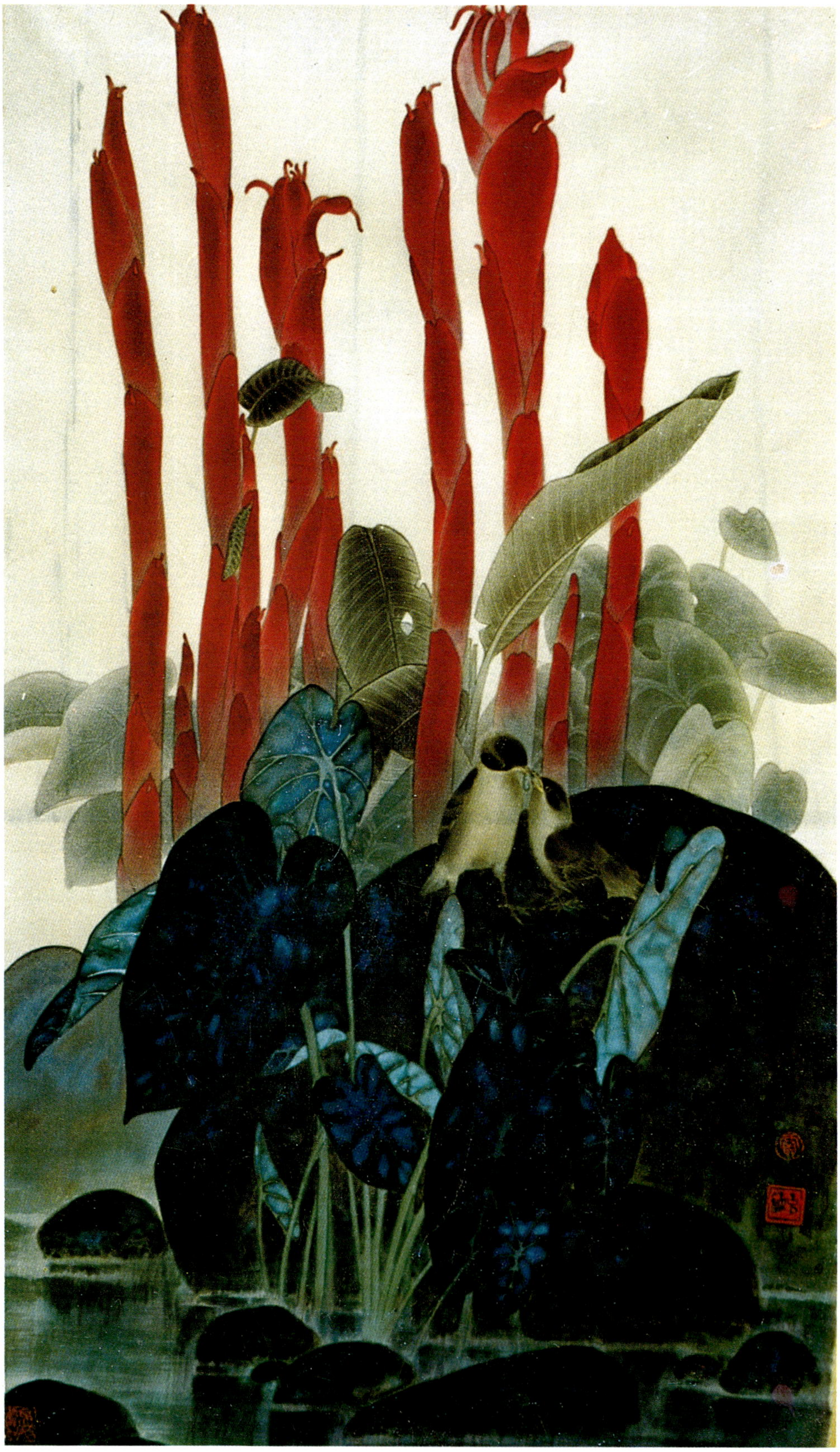

溪畔怀情（1988） 绢本
Feelings by a Creek
50 × 80cm (1988) on silk

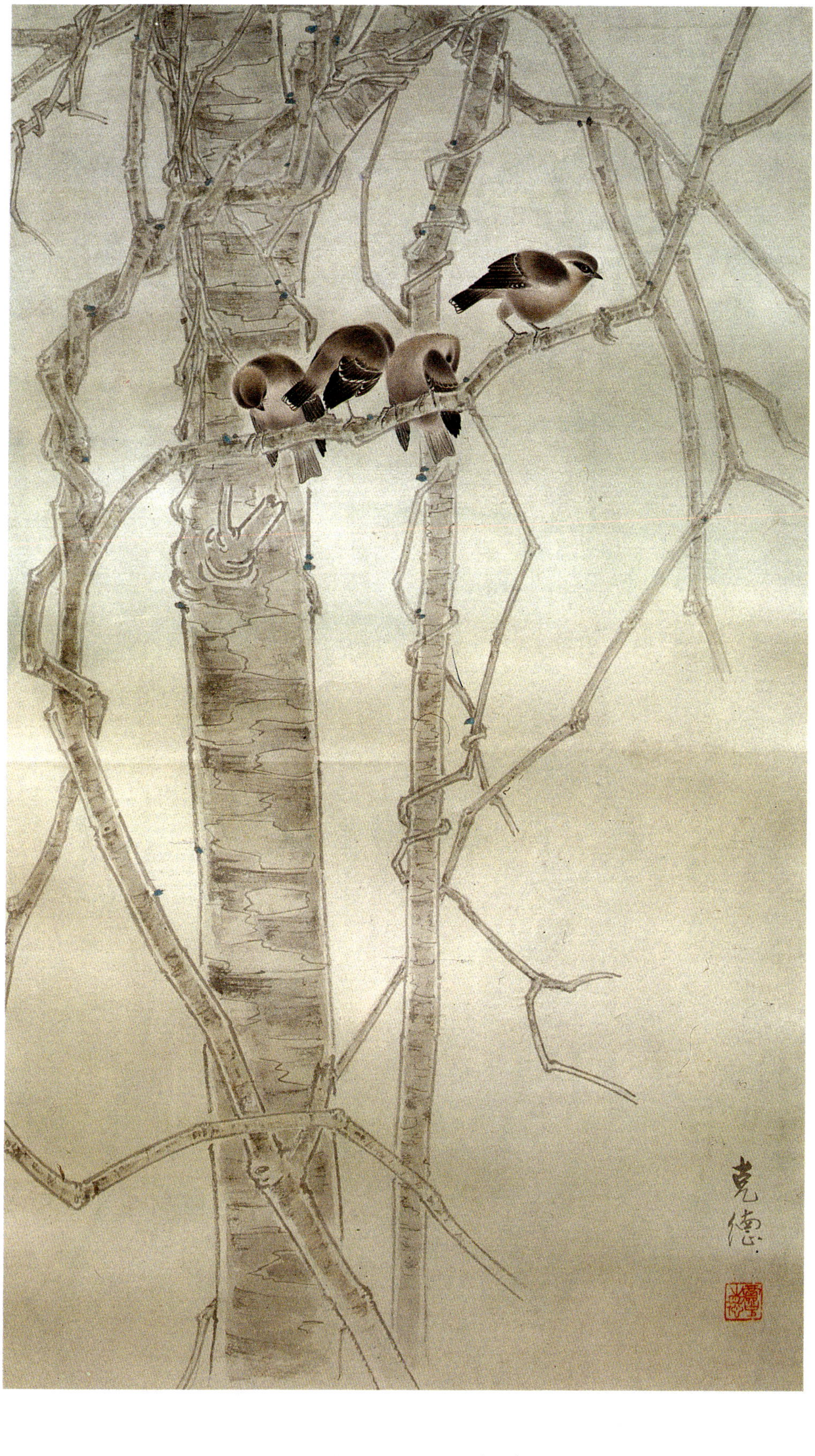

春　晓（1987）　绢本
Morning in Spring
50 × 80cm (1987) on silk

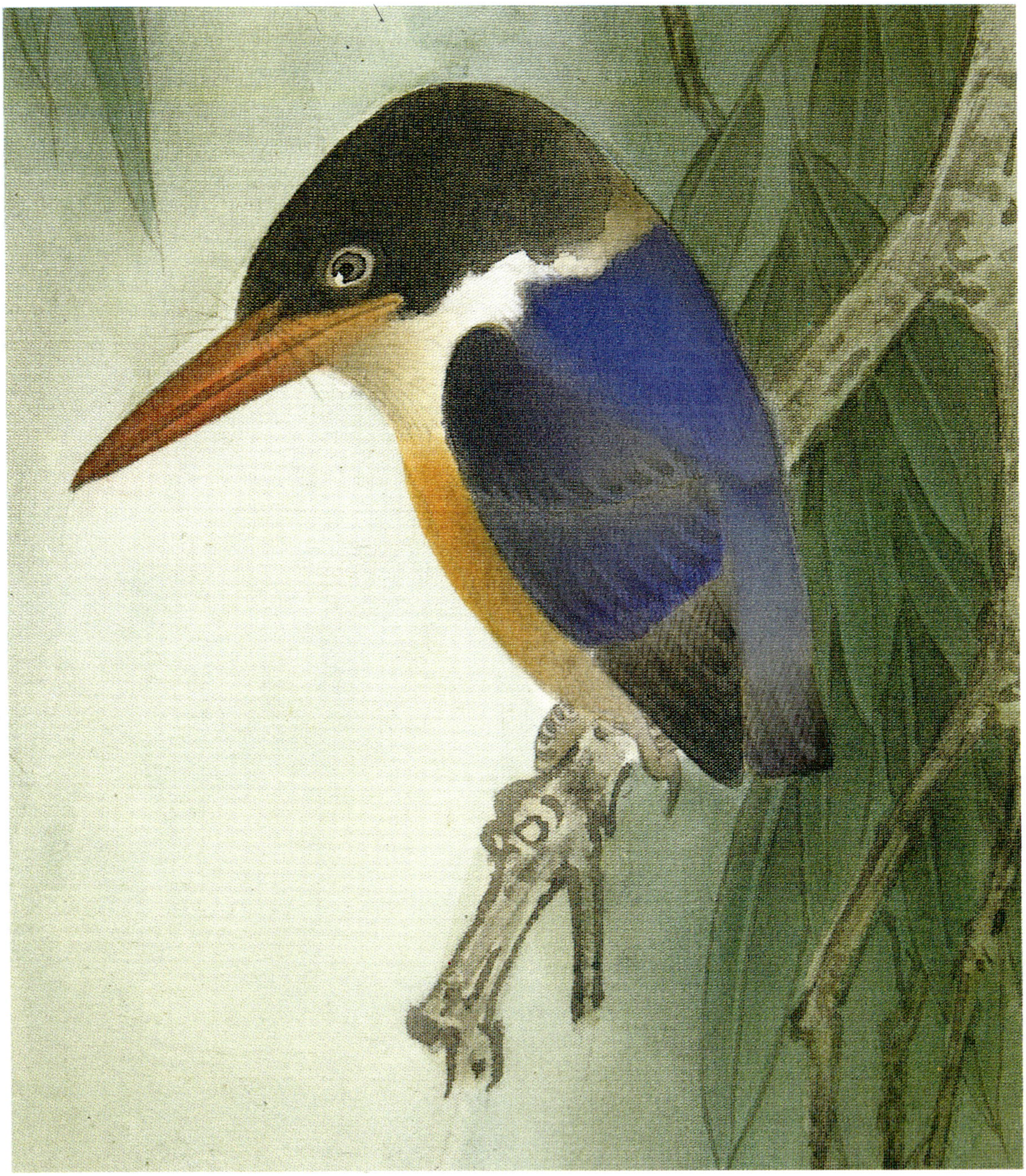

烟雨滋绿（局部）（1996） 绢本
Misty Rain Nurtures Green
60 × 70cm (1996) on silk (detail)

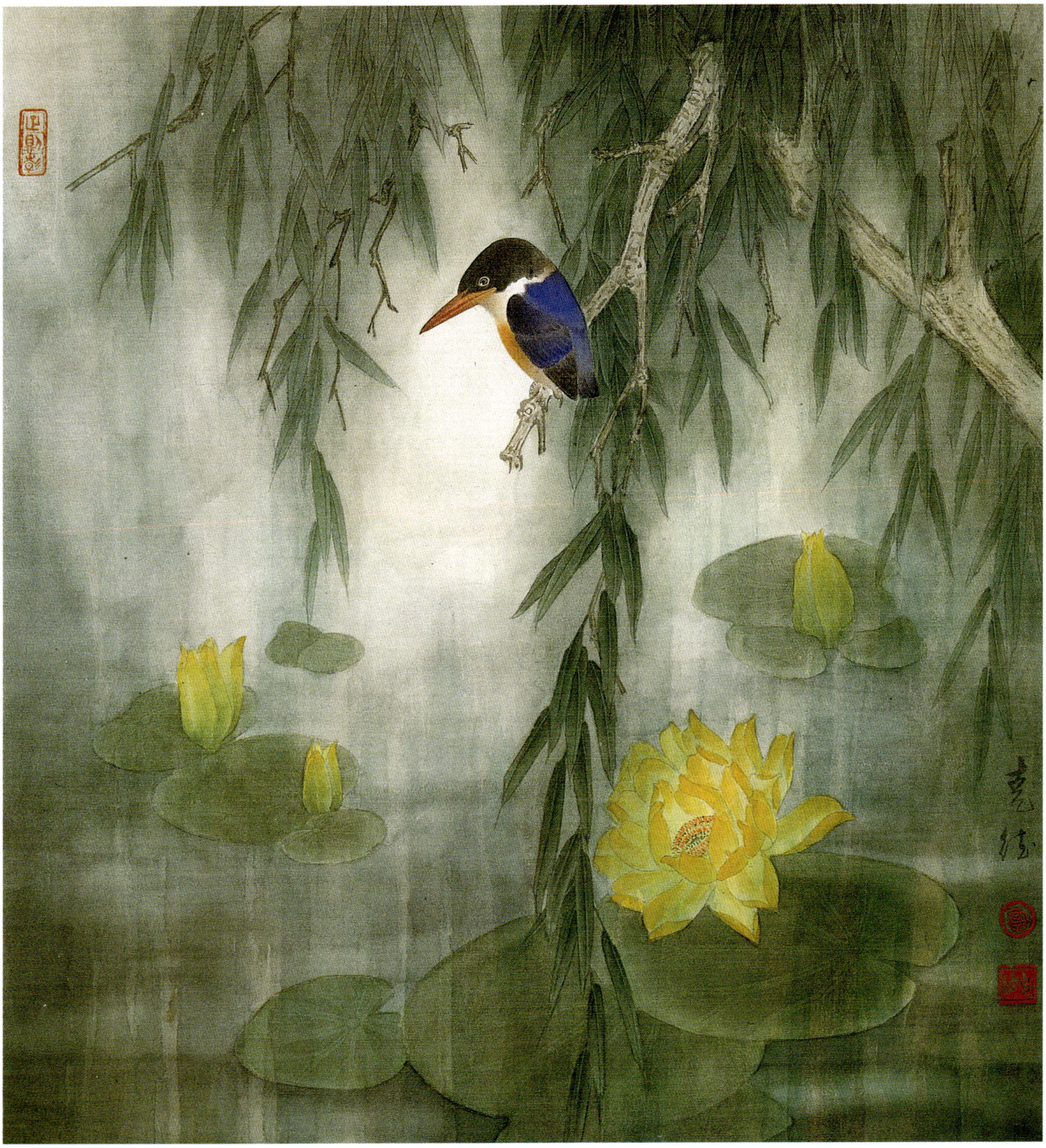

烟雨滋绿（1996） 绢本
Misty Rain Nurtures Green
60 × 70cm (1996) on silk

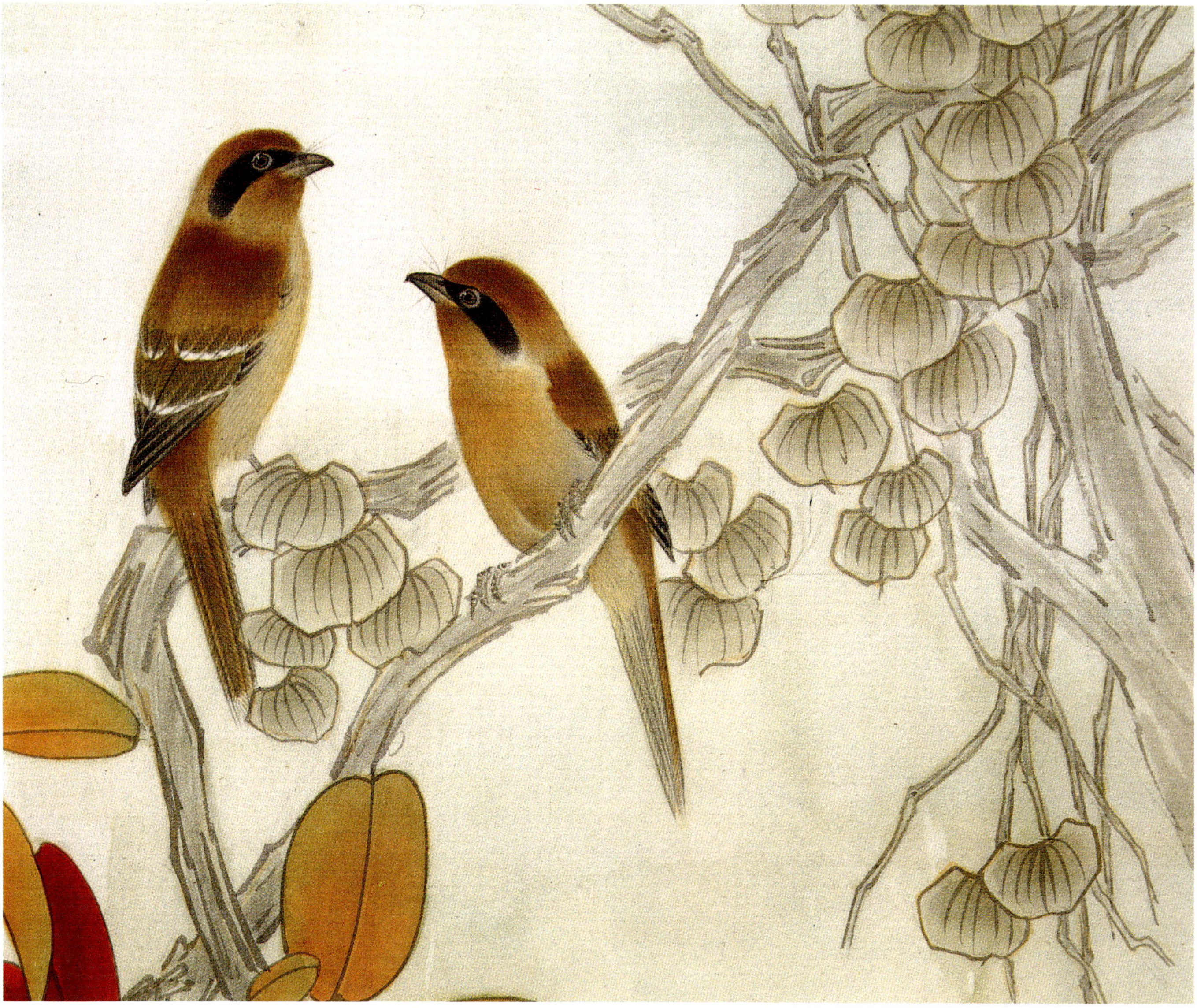

秋　　林（局部）（1996）　绢本
Trees in Autumn
45 × 80cm (1996) on silk (detail)

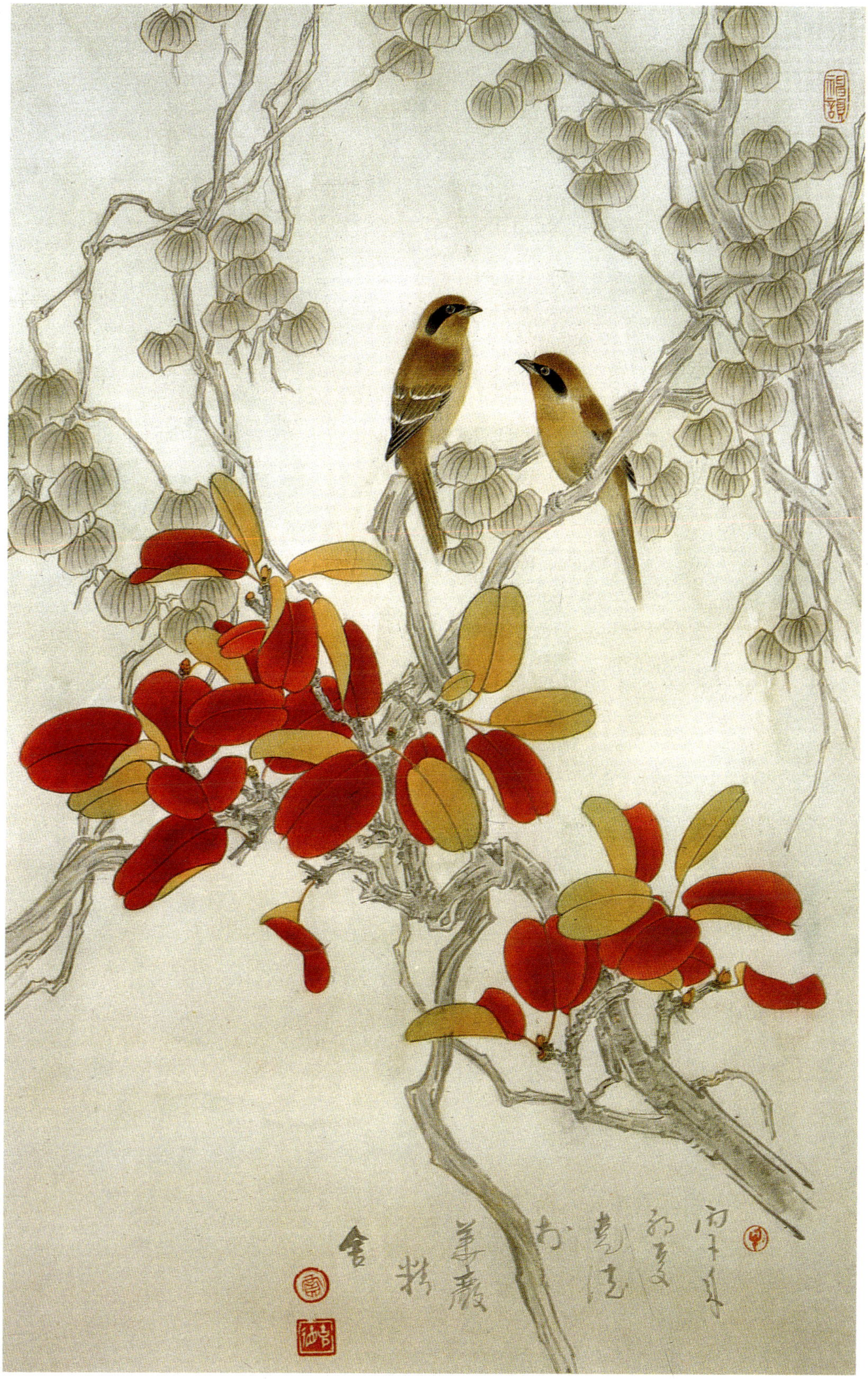

秋　　林（1996）　绢本
Trees in Autumn
45 × 80cm (1996) on silk

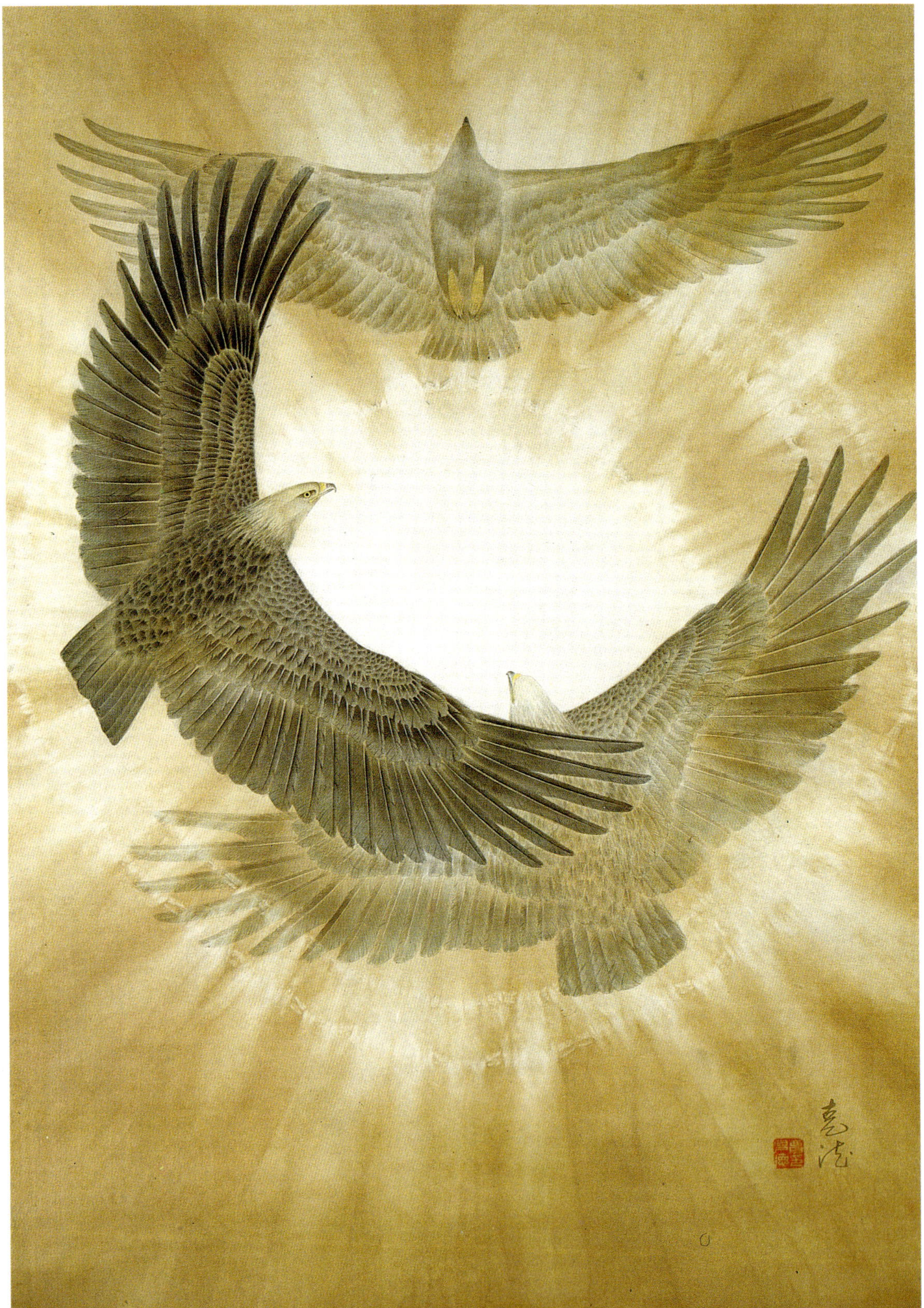

苍　　穹（1989） 绢本
The Vault of Heaven
75 × 130cm (1989) on silk

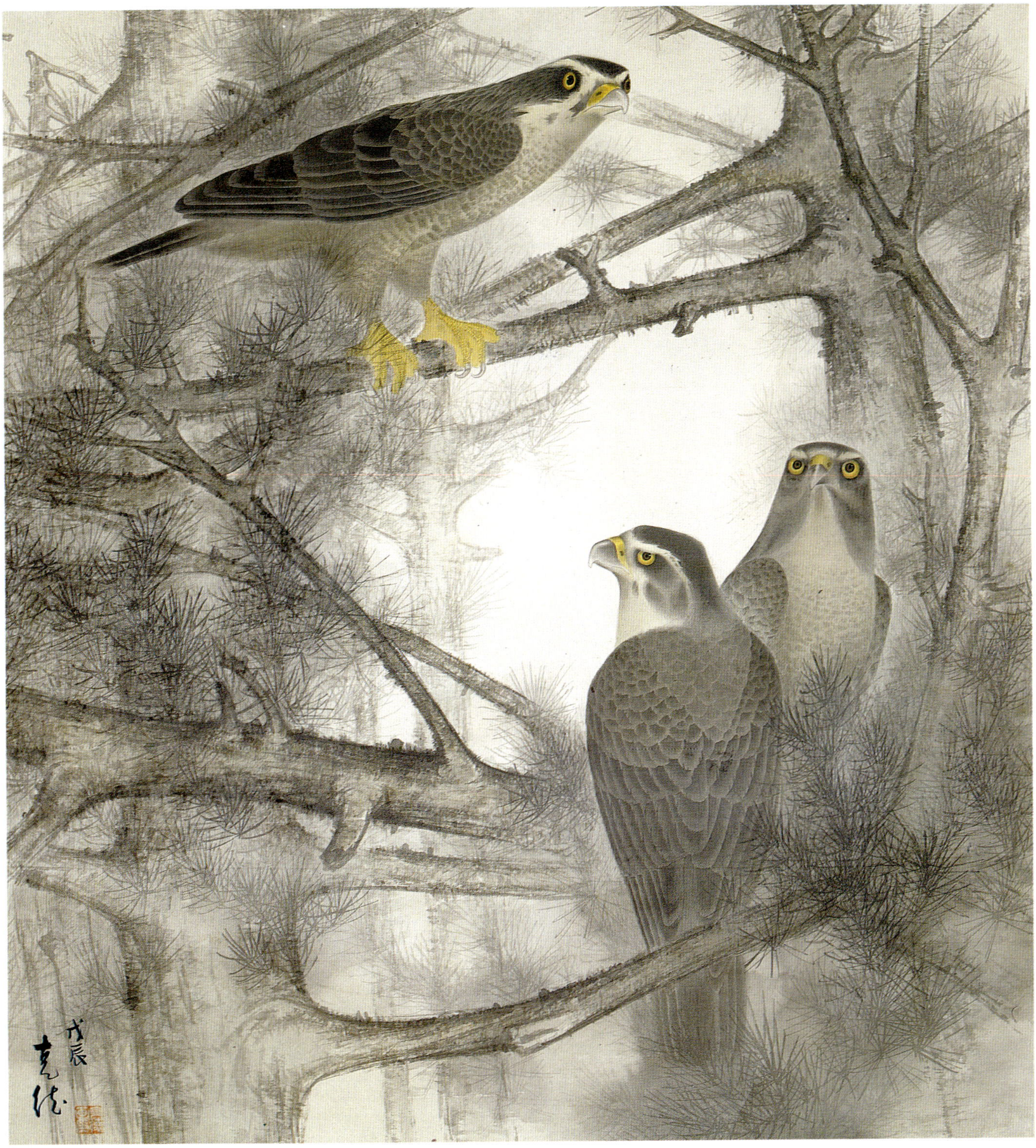

三 英 图（1988） 绢本
Three Eagles
120 × 140cm (1988) on silk

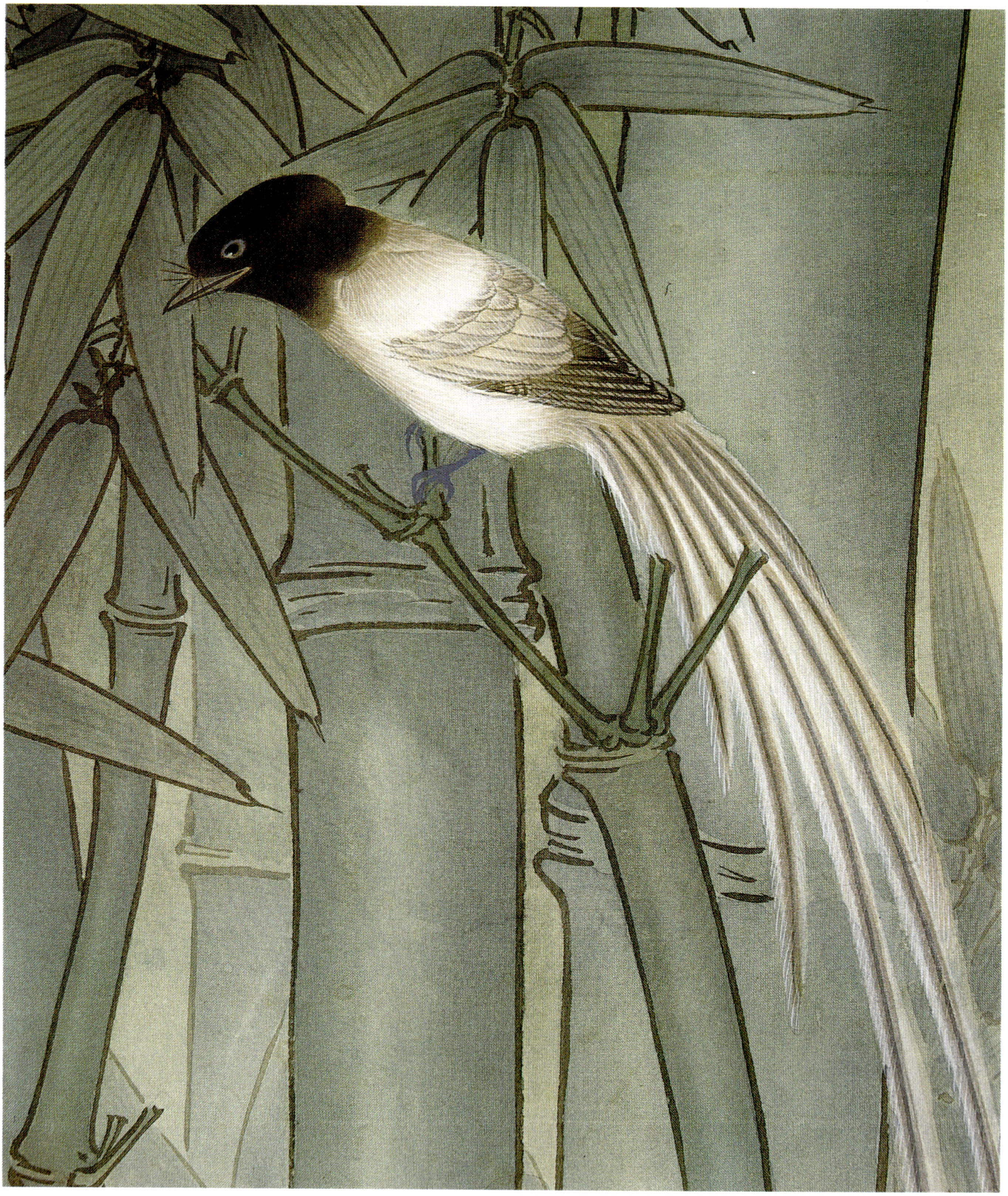

翠竹青青（局部）（1982） 绢本
Luxuriant Bamboo
150 × 80cm (1982) on silk (detail)

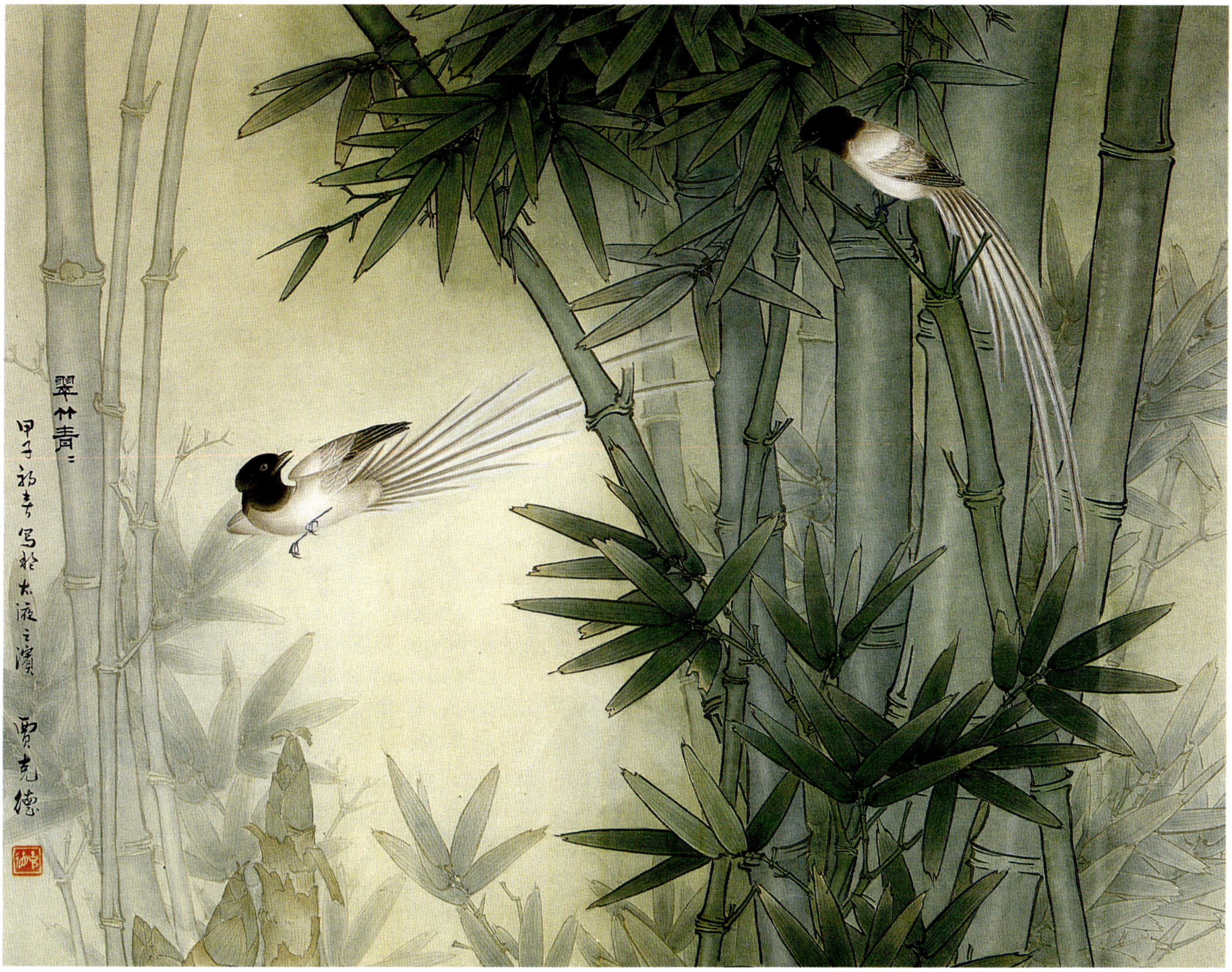

翠竹青青（1982） 绢本
Luxuriant Bamboo
150 × 80cm (1982) on silk

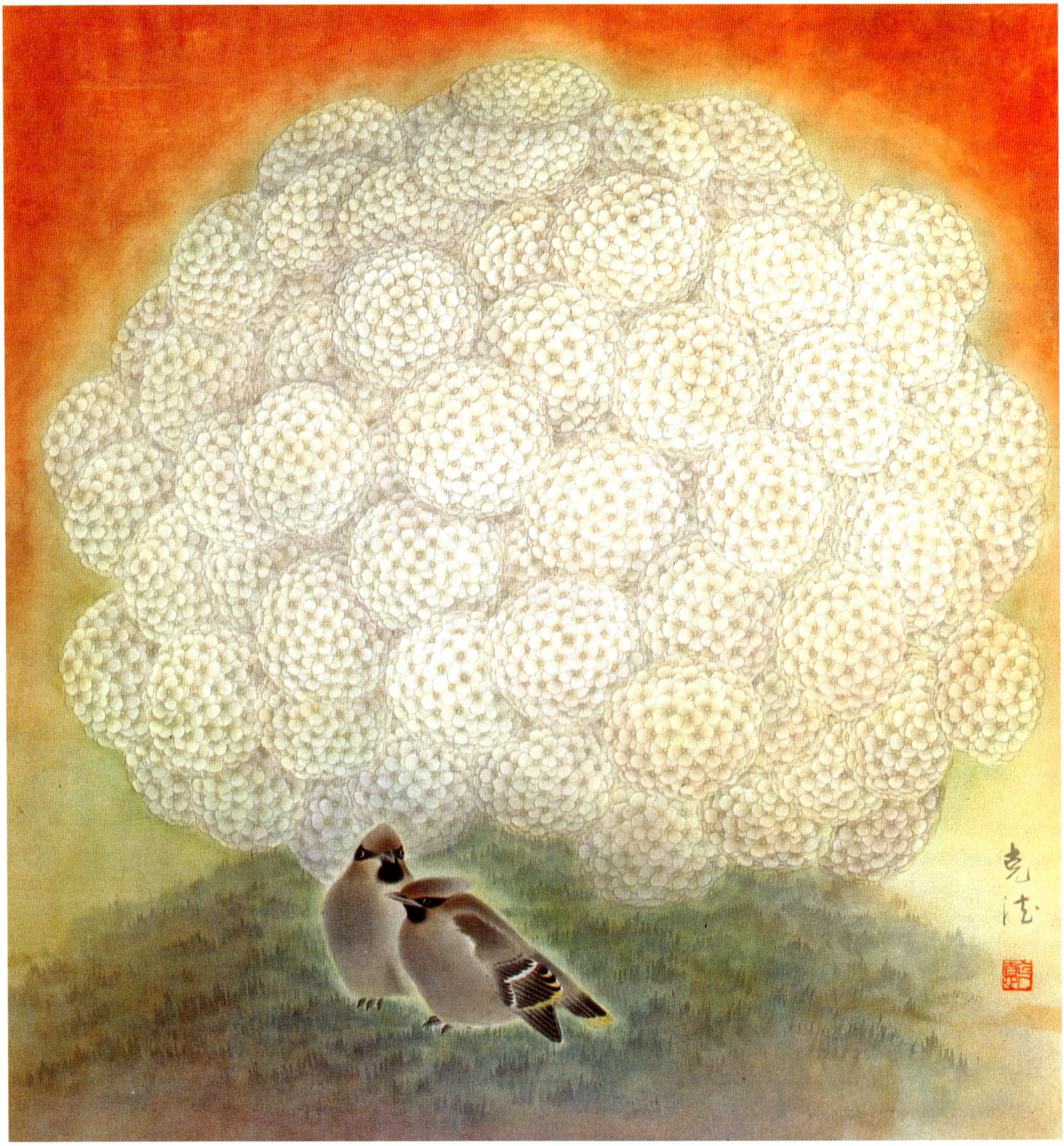

太平春光（1995） 绢本
Peaceful Spring
85 × 85cm (1995) on silk

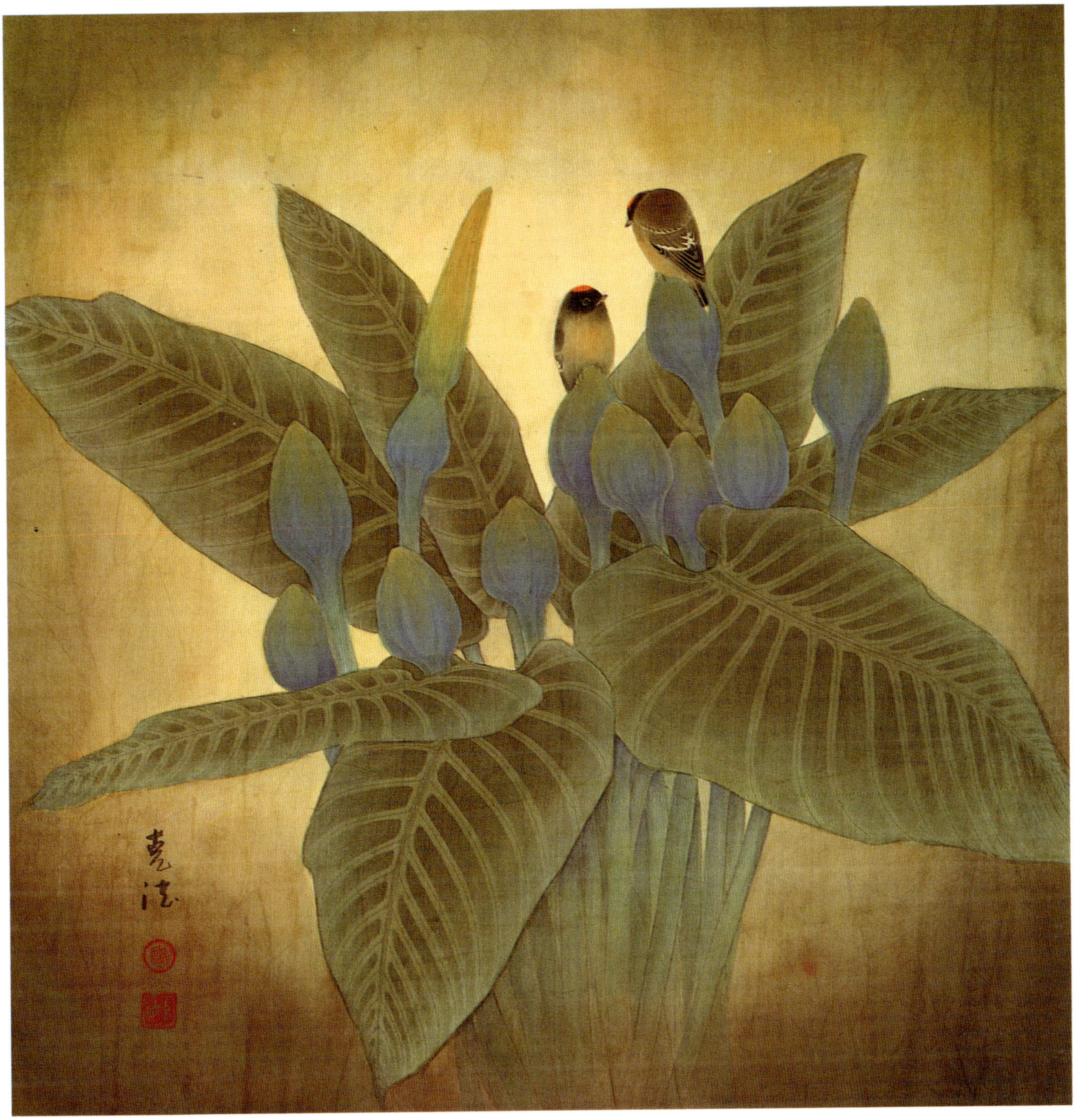

留红点翠（1996） 绢本
Red and Green
80 × 80cm (1996) on silk

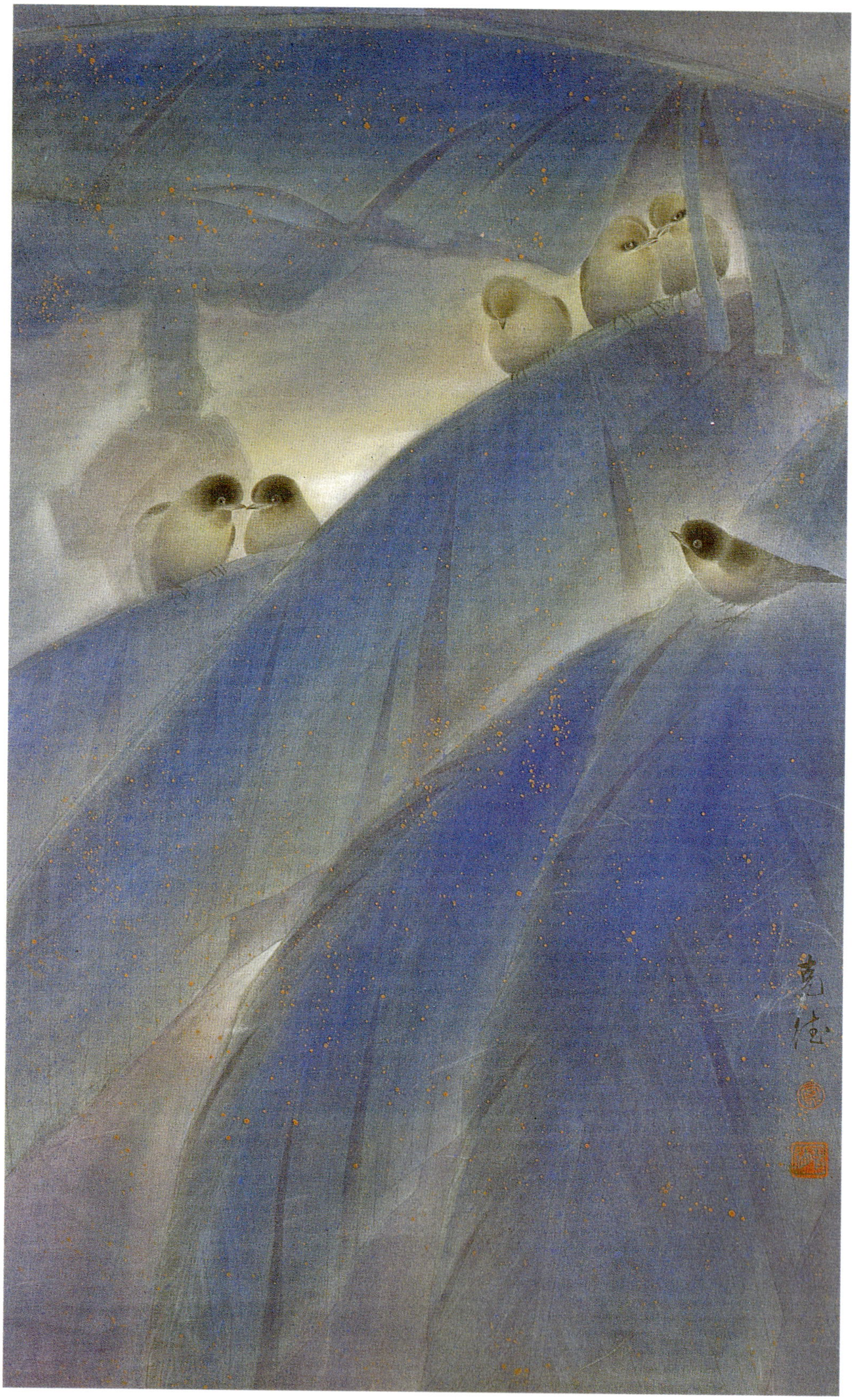

蕉林春雨（1992） 绢本
Spring Rain Over a Palm Grove
45 × 60cm (1992) on silk

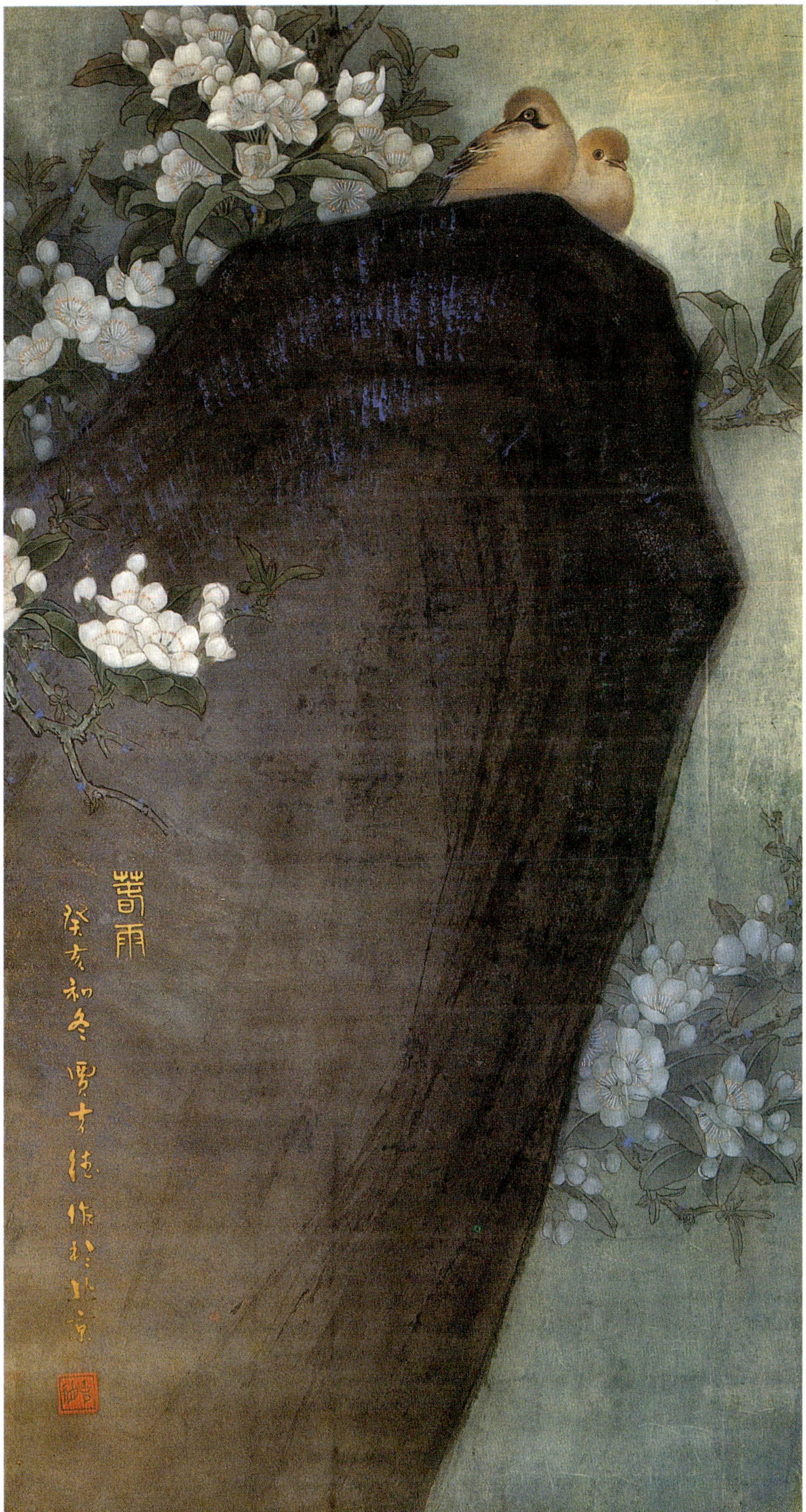

春　　雨（1981）　纸本

Spring Rain

45 × 90cm (1981) on paper

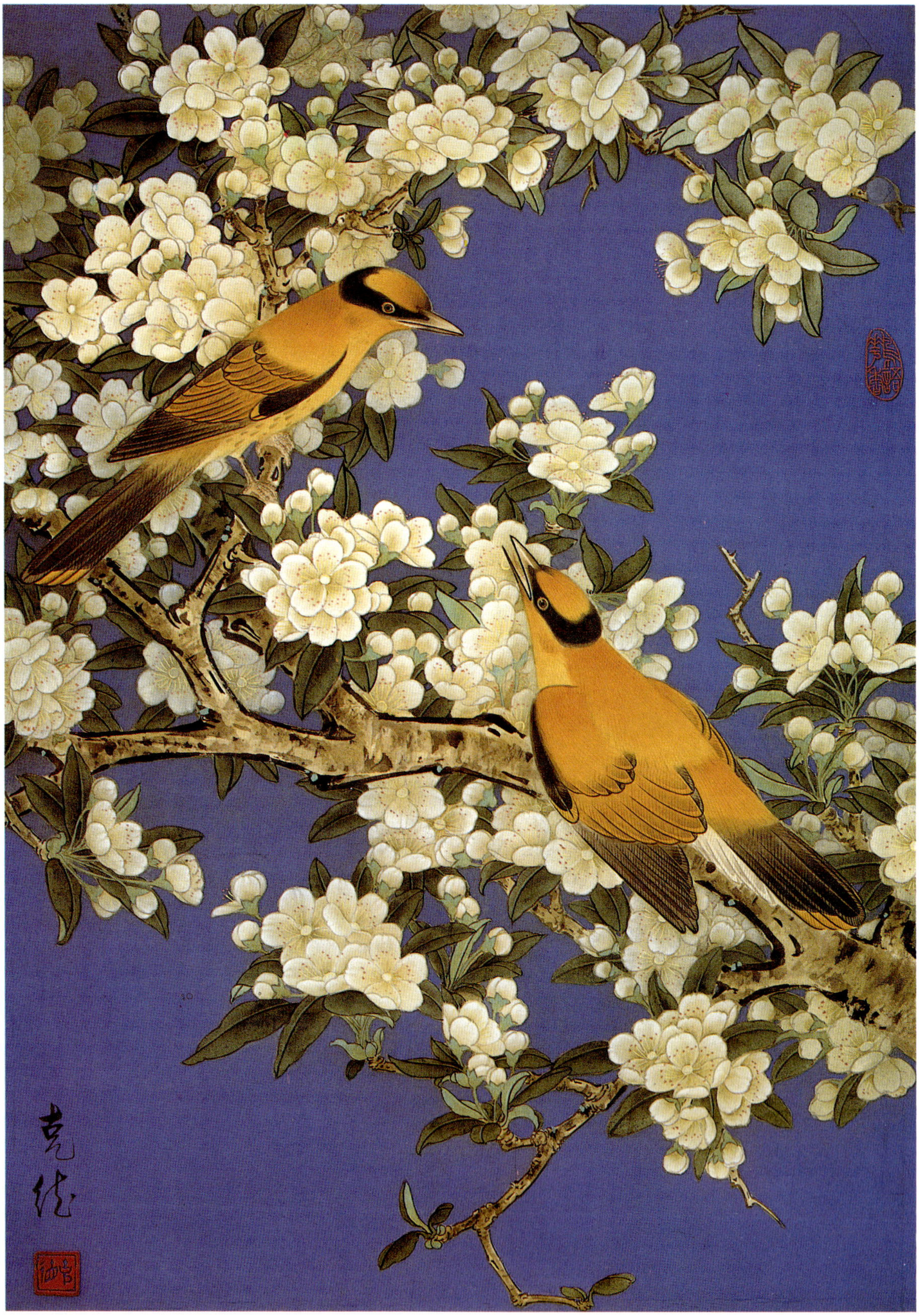

泛　　春（1980）　纸本
Rich Spring
50 × 80cm (1980) on paper

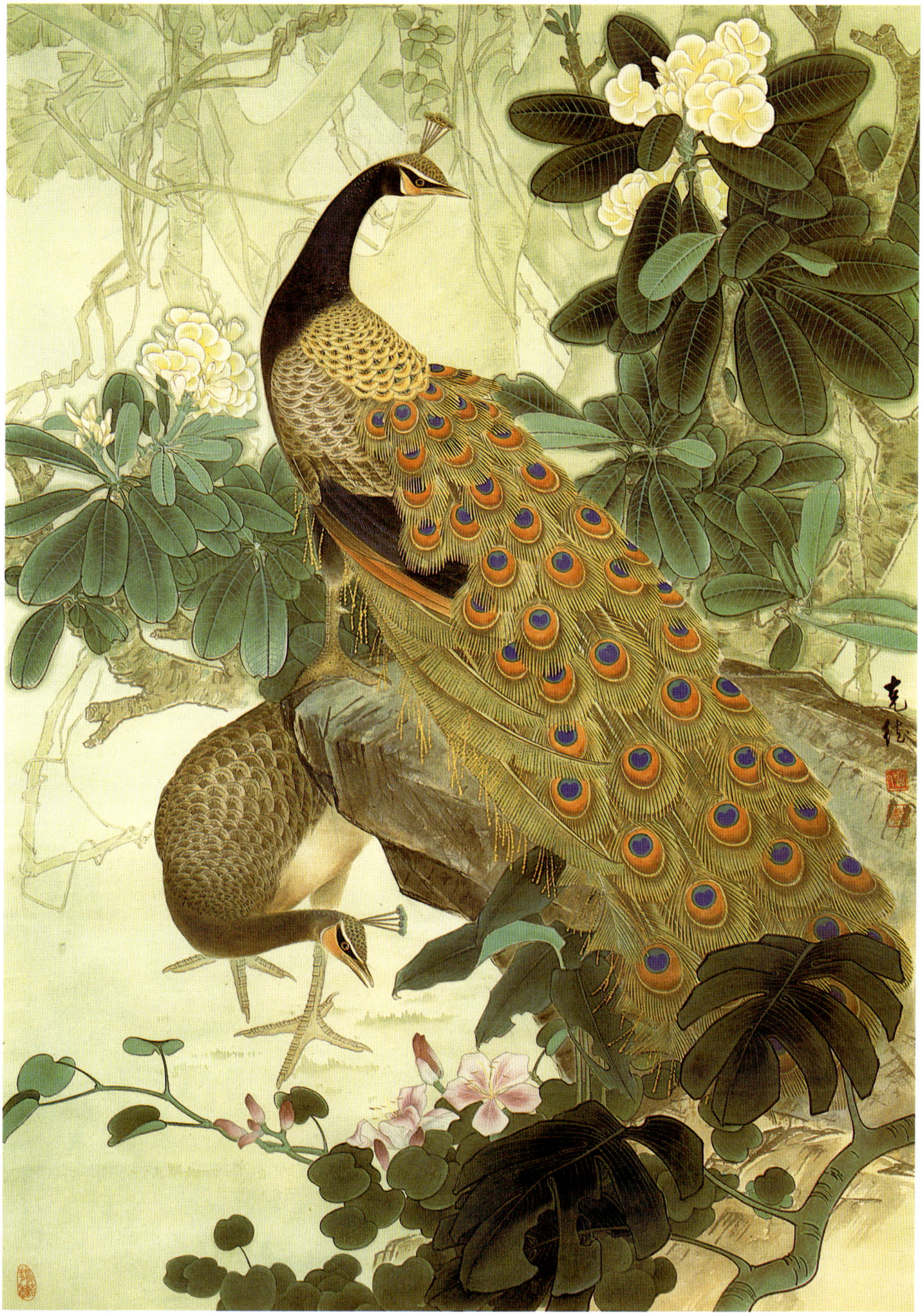

锦绣丽质（1984） 绢本
Exquisite Beauty
80 × 130cm (1984) on silk

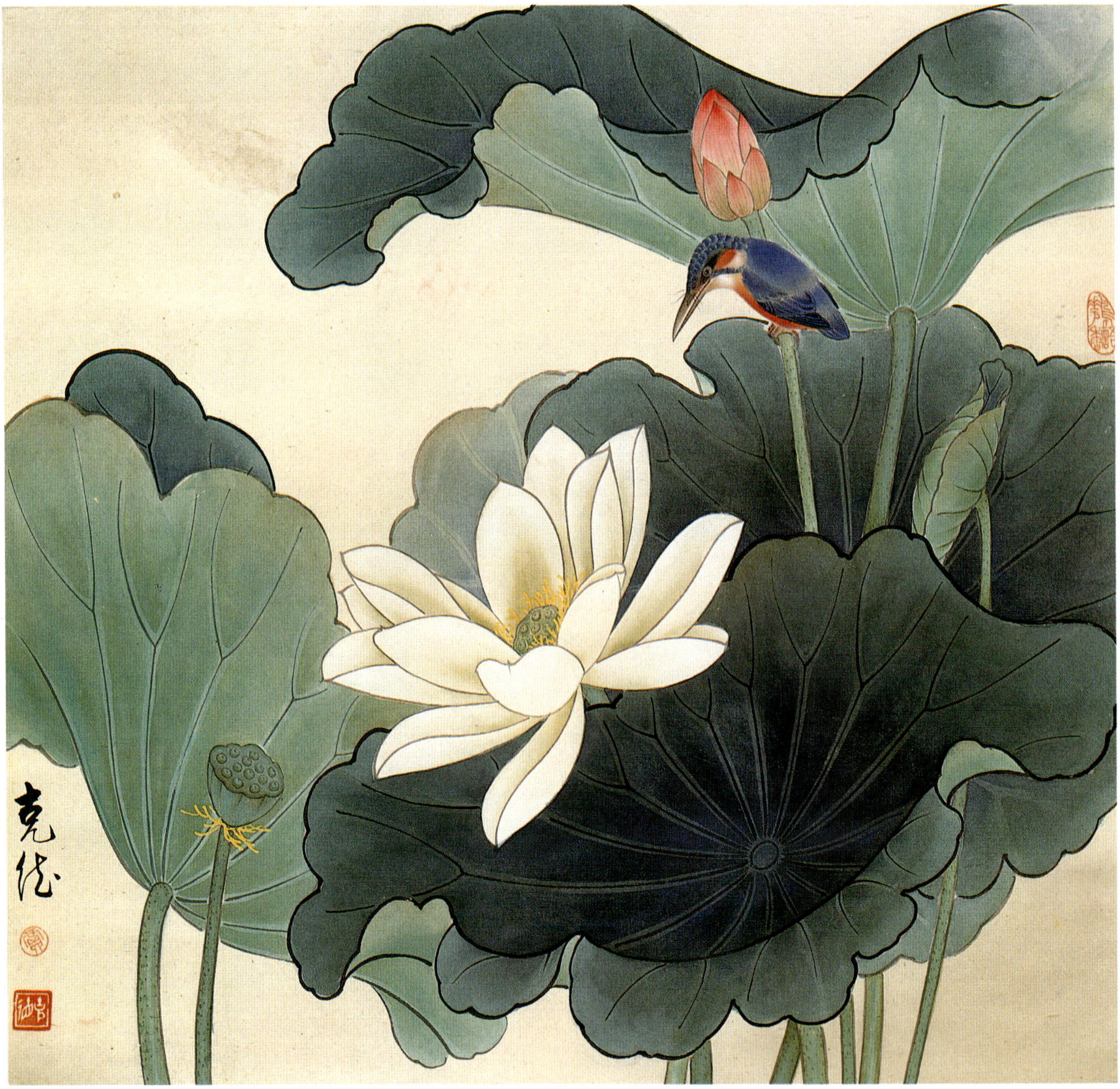

白　　荷（1982）　绢本
White Lotus
60 × 60cm (1982) on silk

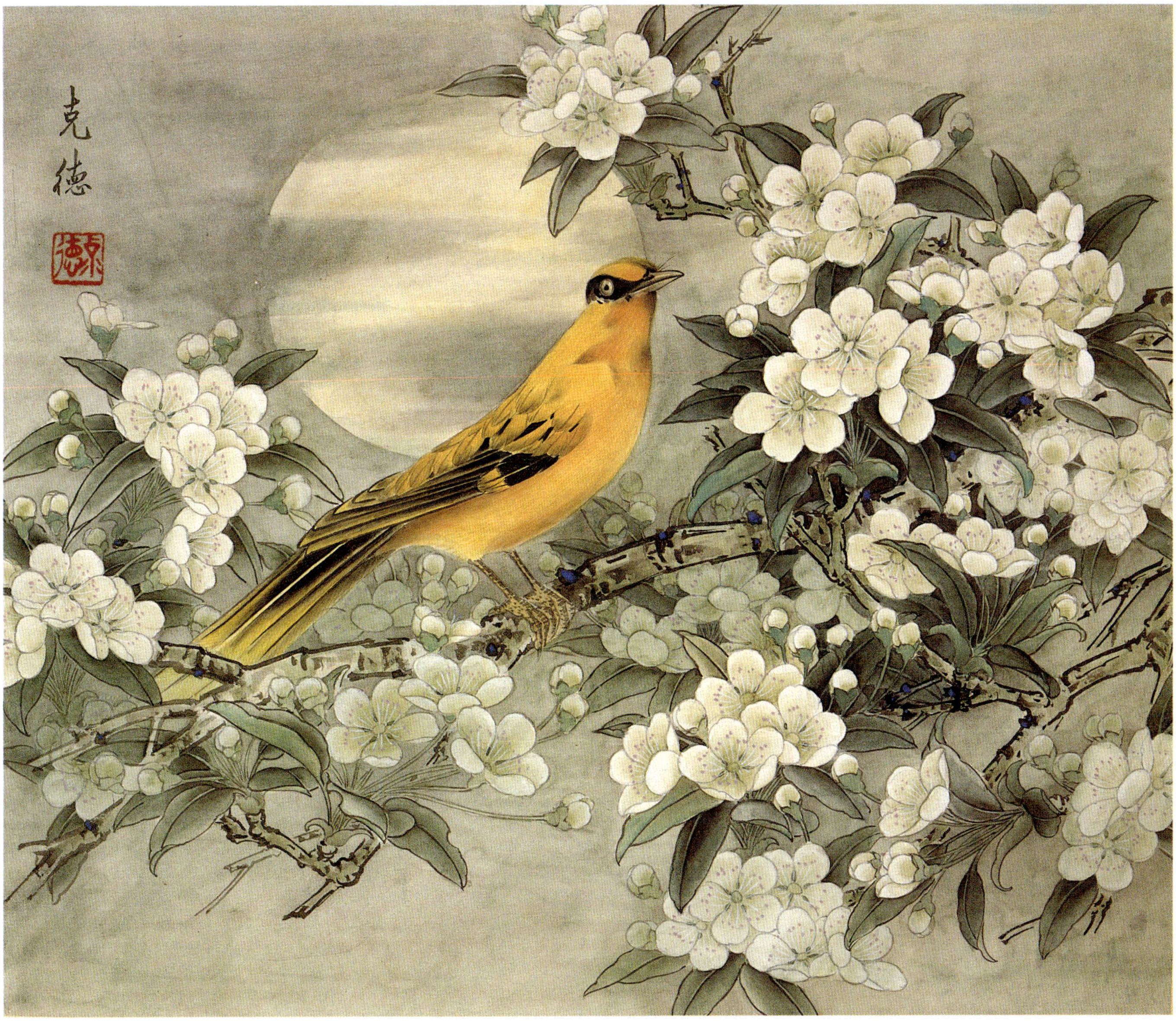

春　　静（1980）　绢本
Tranquility in Spring
40 × 35cm (1980) on silk

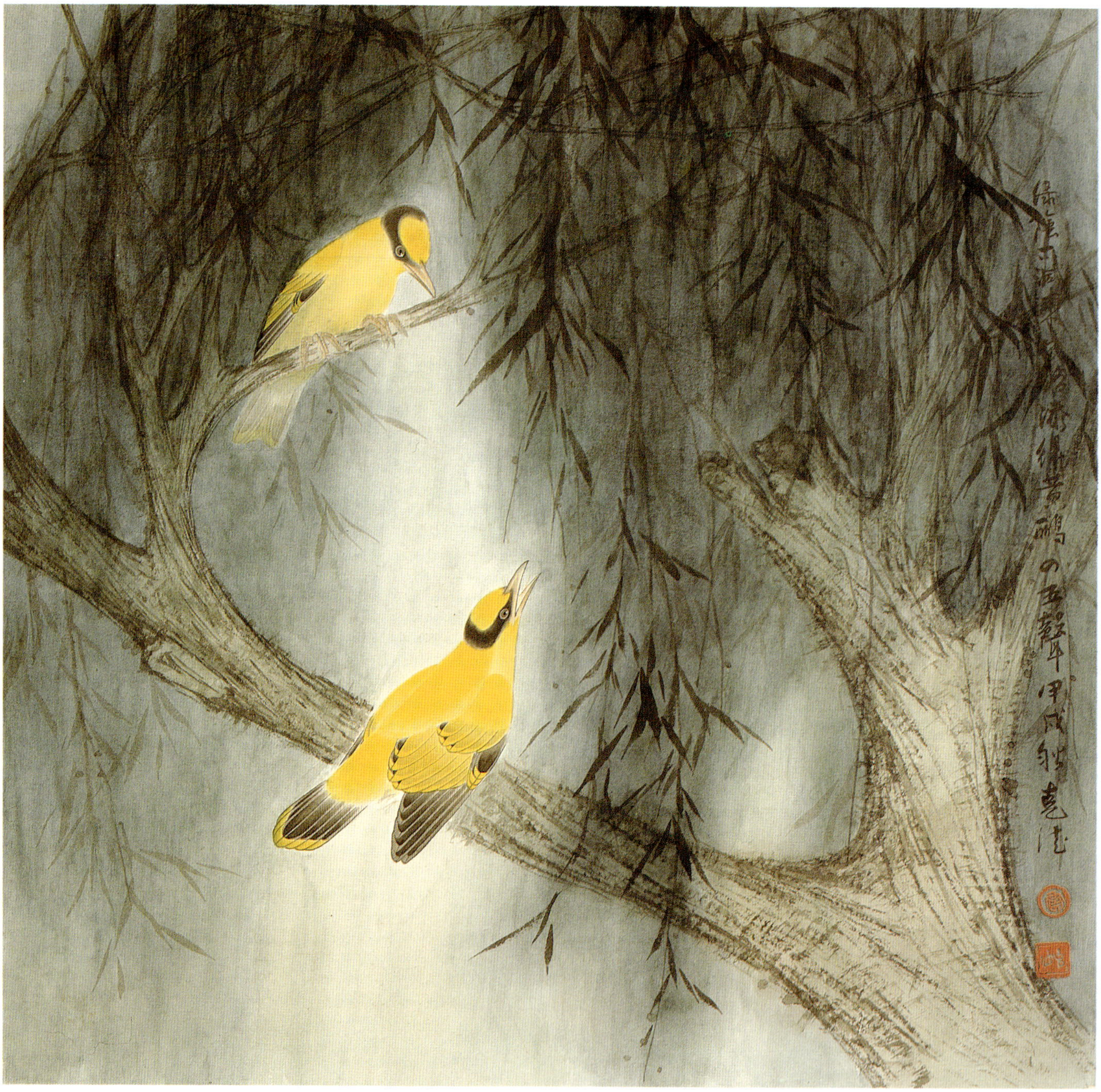

柳　　荫（1986） 绢本
In the Shade of Willow
60 × 60cm (1986) on silk

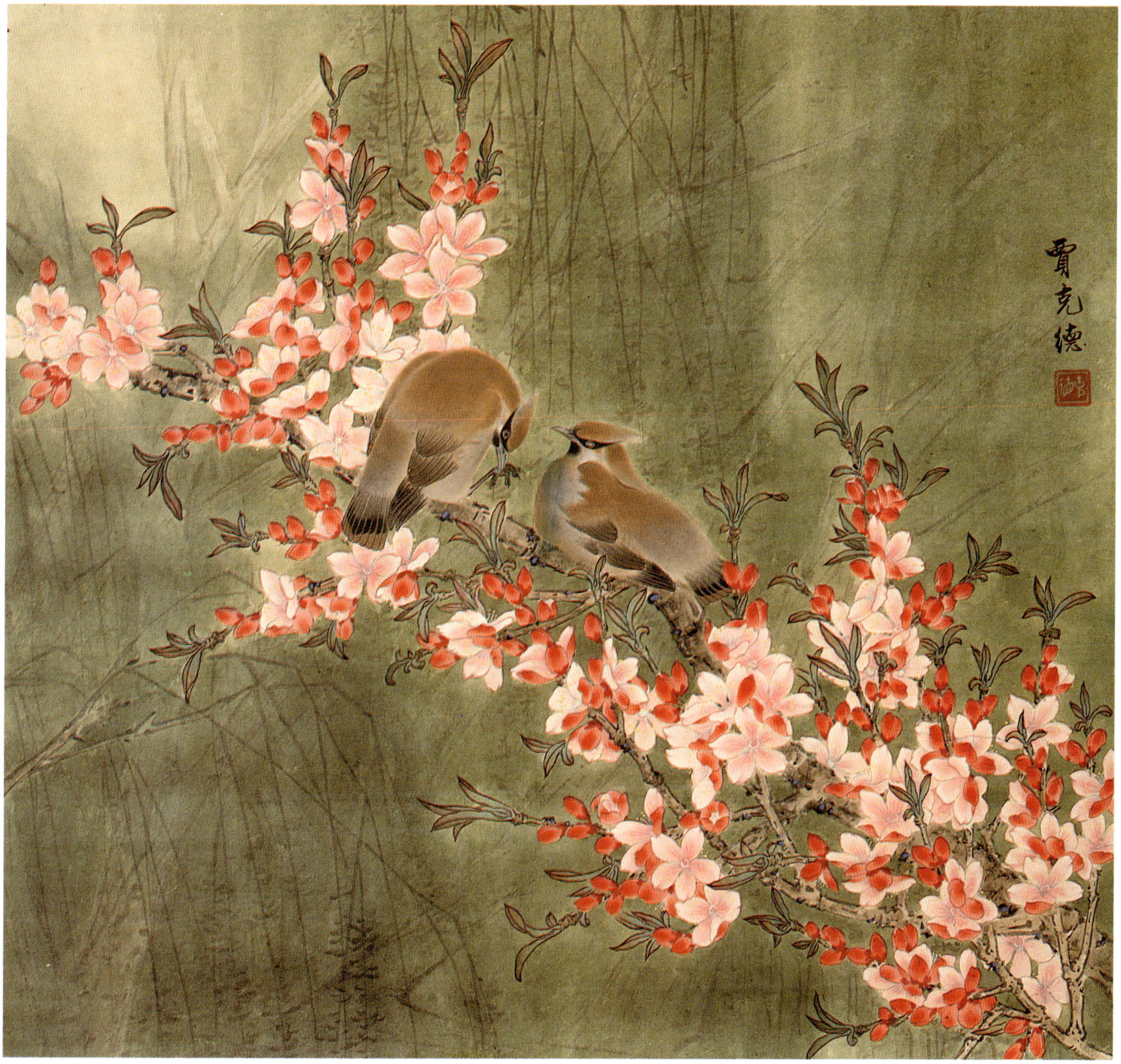

桃红又是一年春（1979） 绢本
Blooming Peaches Herald a New Spring
60 × 60cm (1979) on silk

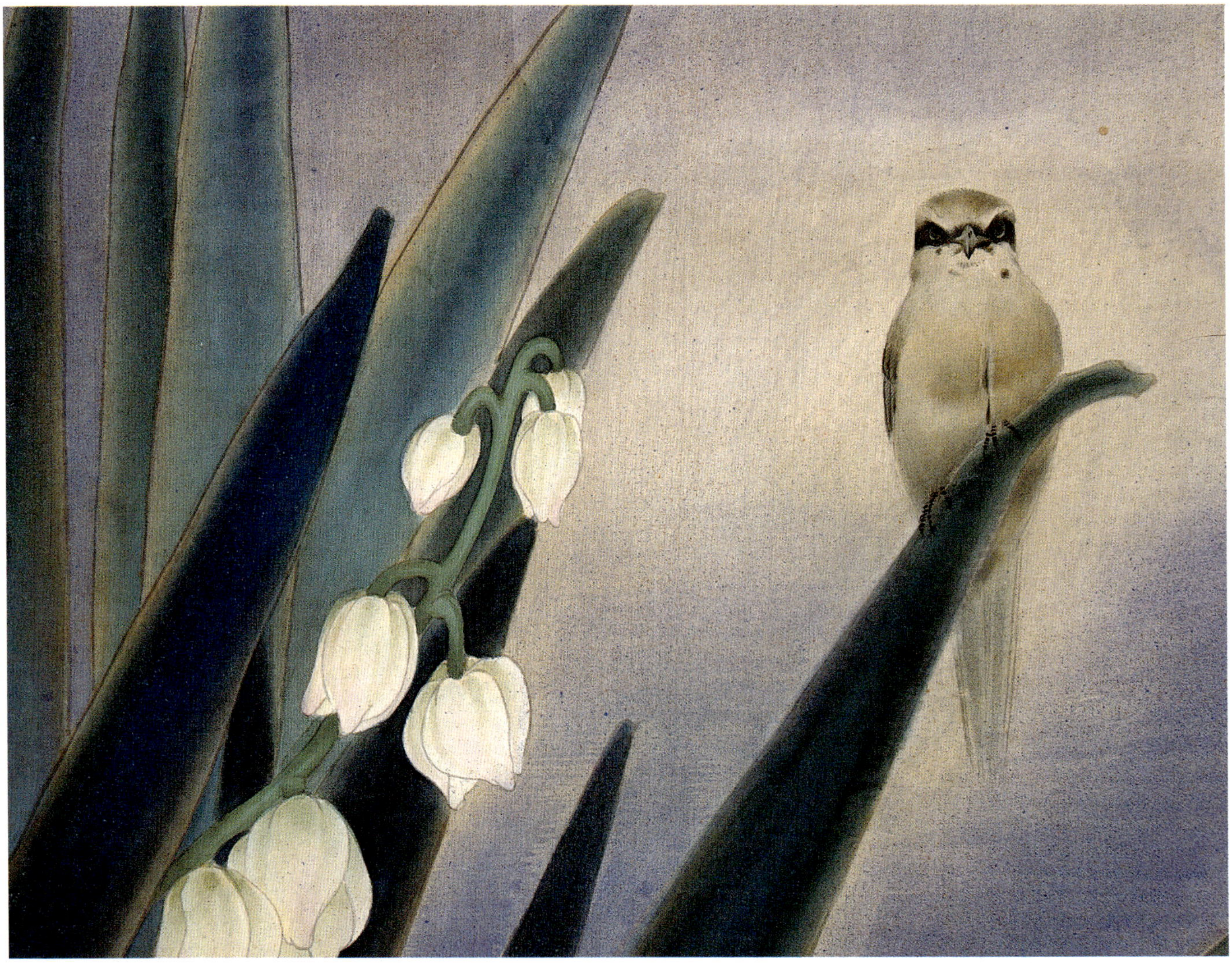

润含春雨（1990） 绢本
In Misty Spring Rain
86 × 86cm (1990) on silk (detail)

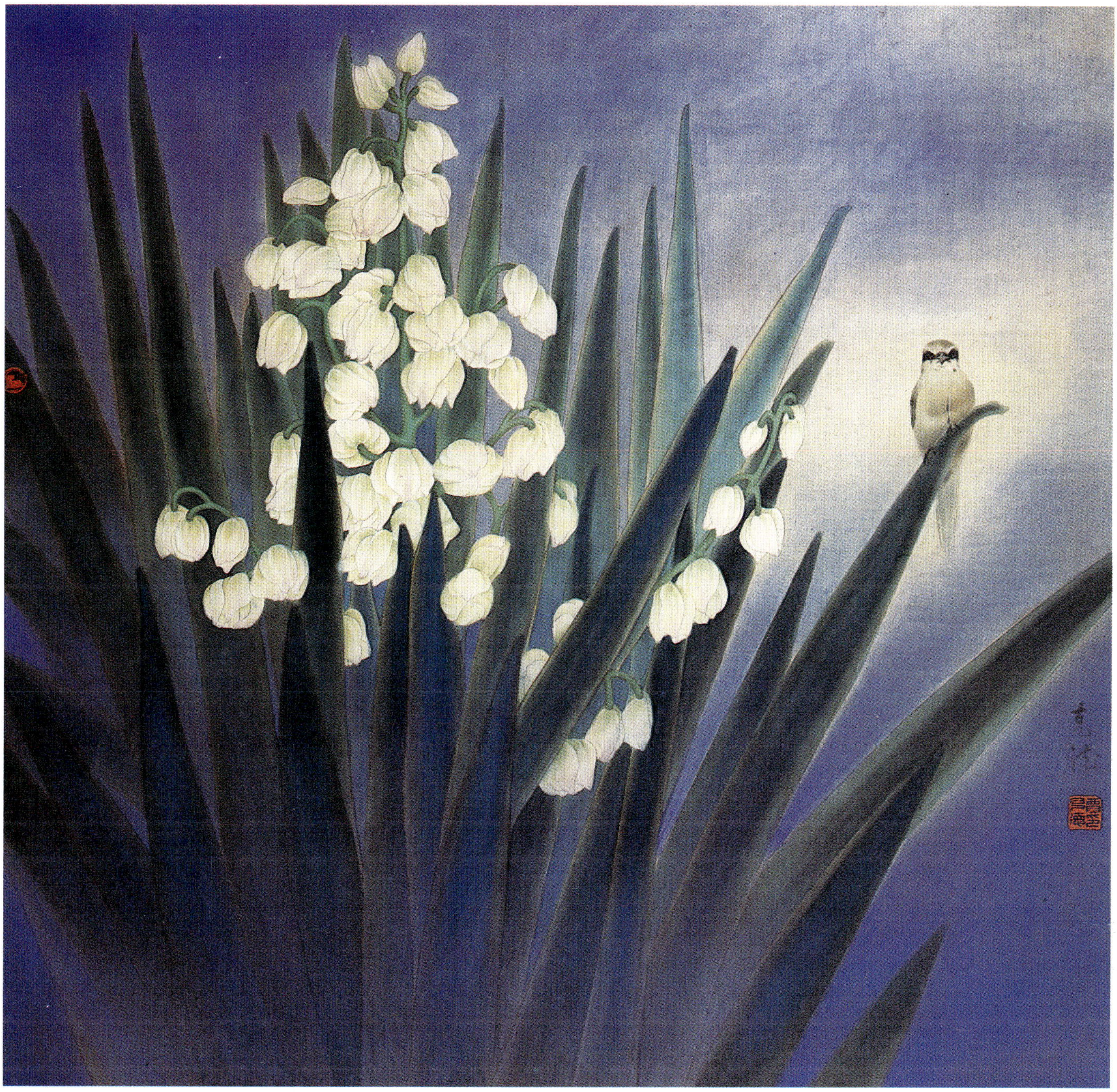

润含春雨（1990） 绢本
In Misty Spring Rain
86 × 86cm (1990) on silk

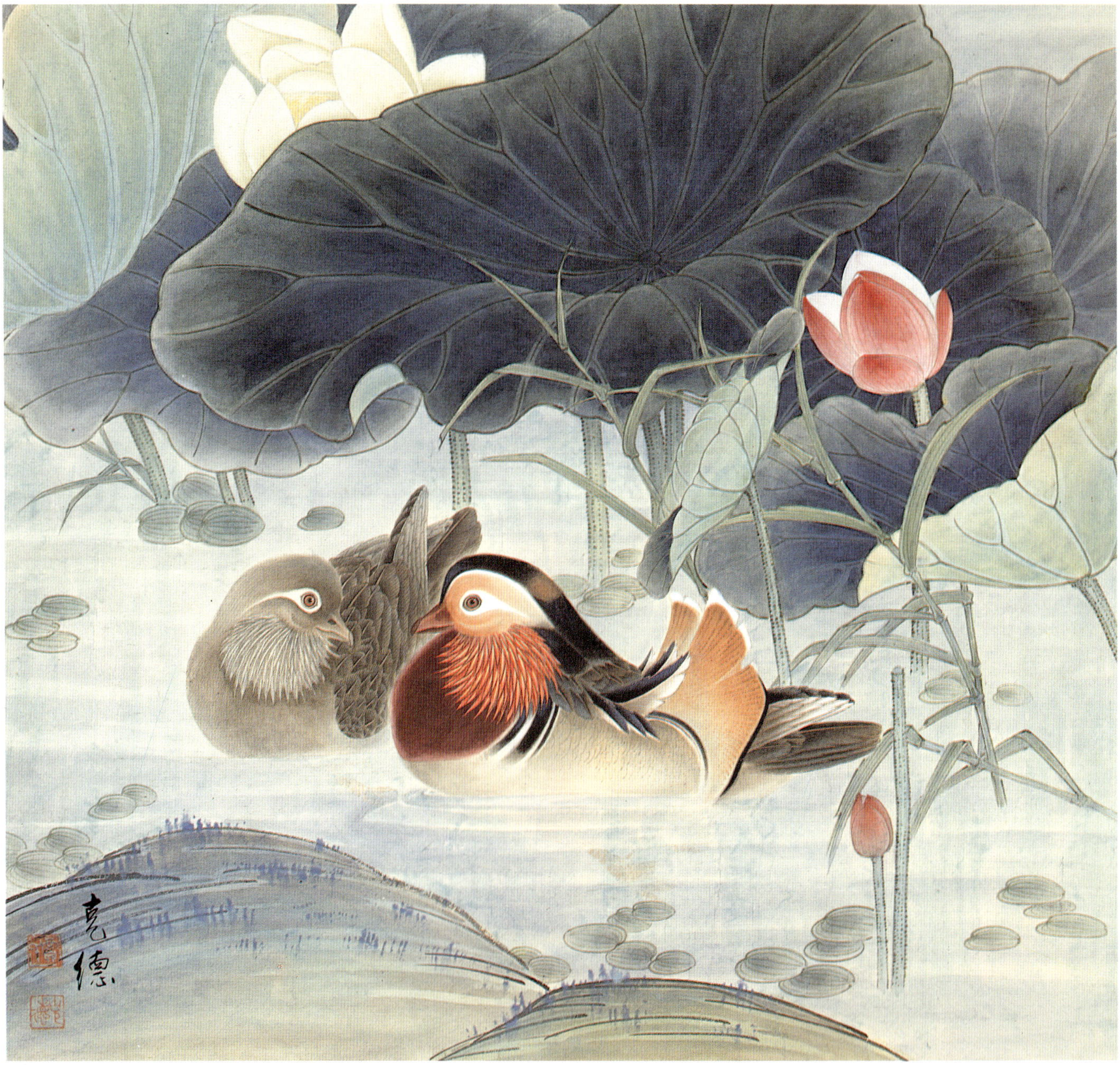

荷花鸳鸯（1982） 纸本
Lotus and Mandarin Ducks
50 × 50cm (1982) on paper

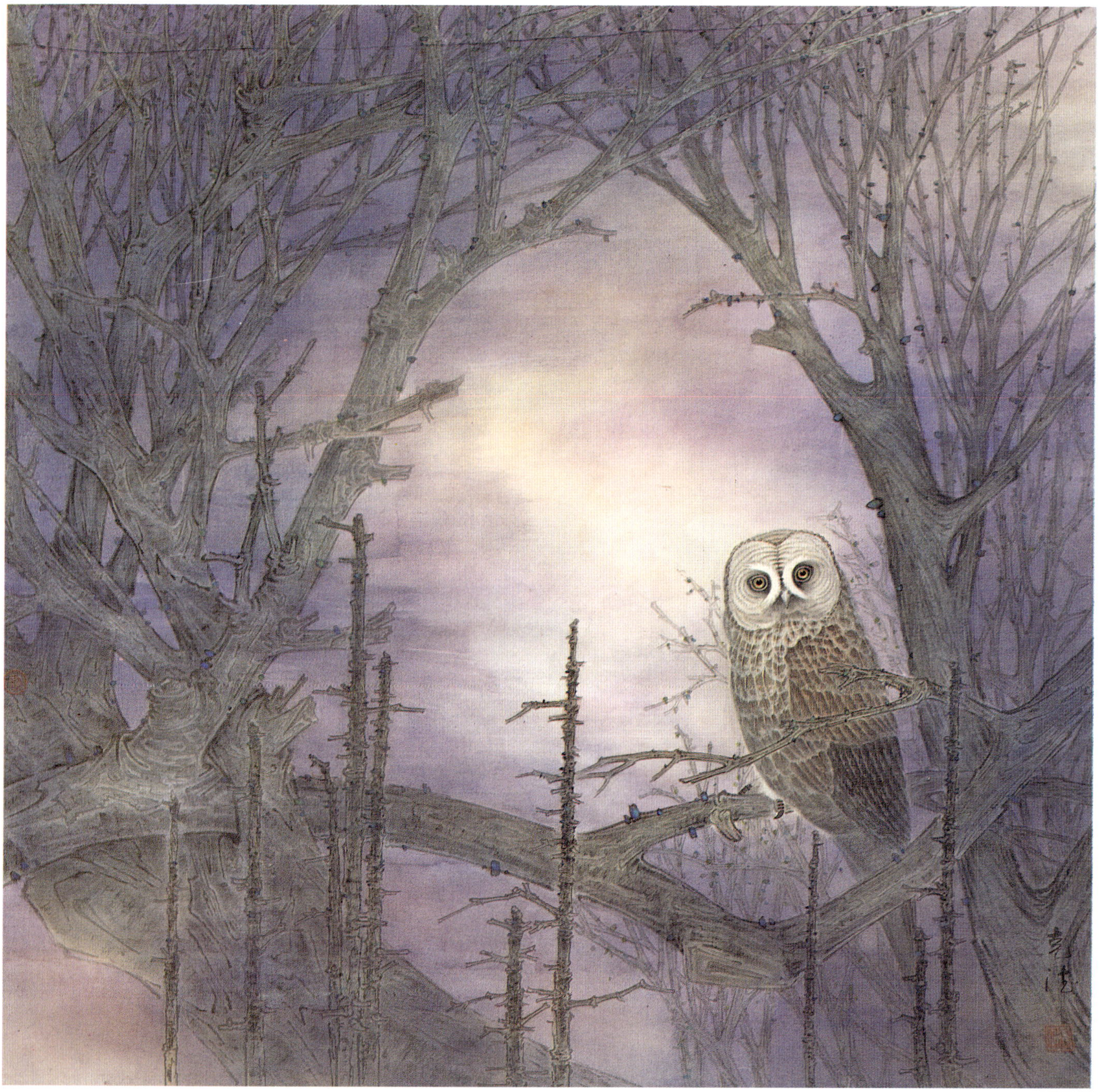

老树无丑枝（1989） 绢本
An Old Tree Without Ugly Branches
75×75cm (1989) on silk

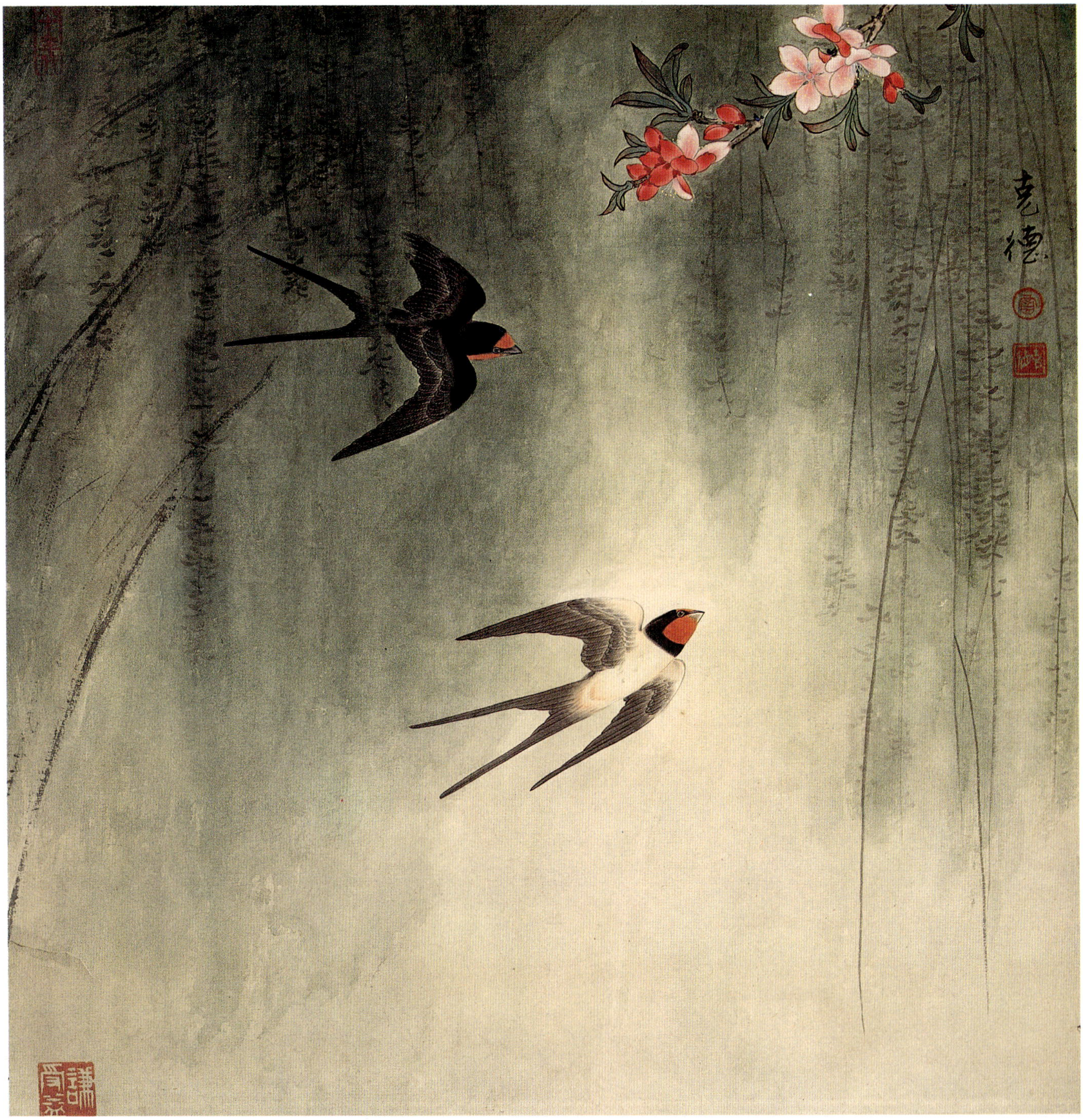

柳荫双燕（1979） 绢本
Twin Swallows and Willow
60 × 60cm (1979) on paper

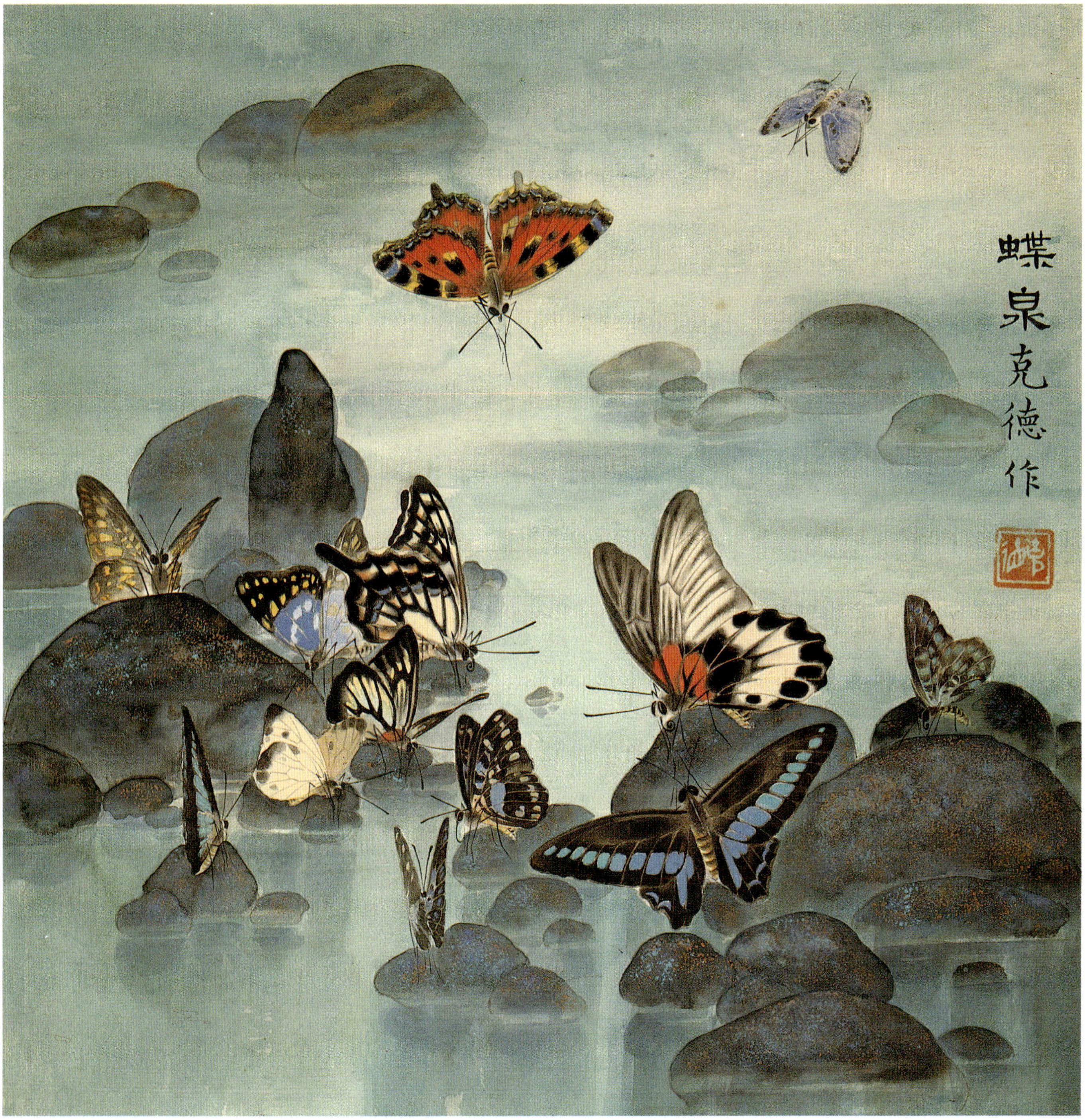

蝶　　泉（1983）　绢本
Butterflies by a Spring
45 × 45cm (1983) on silk

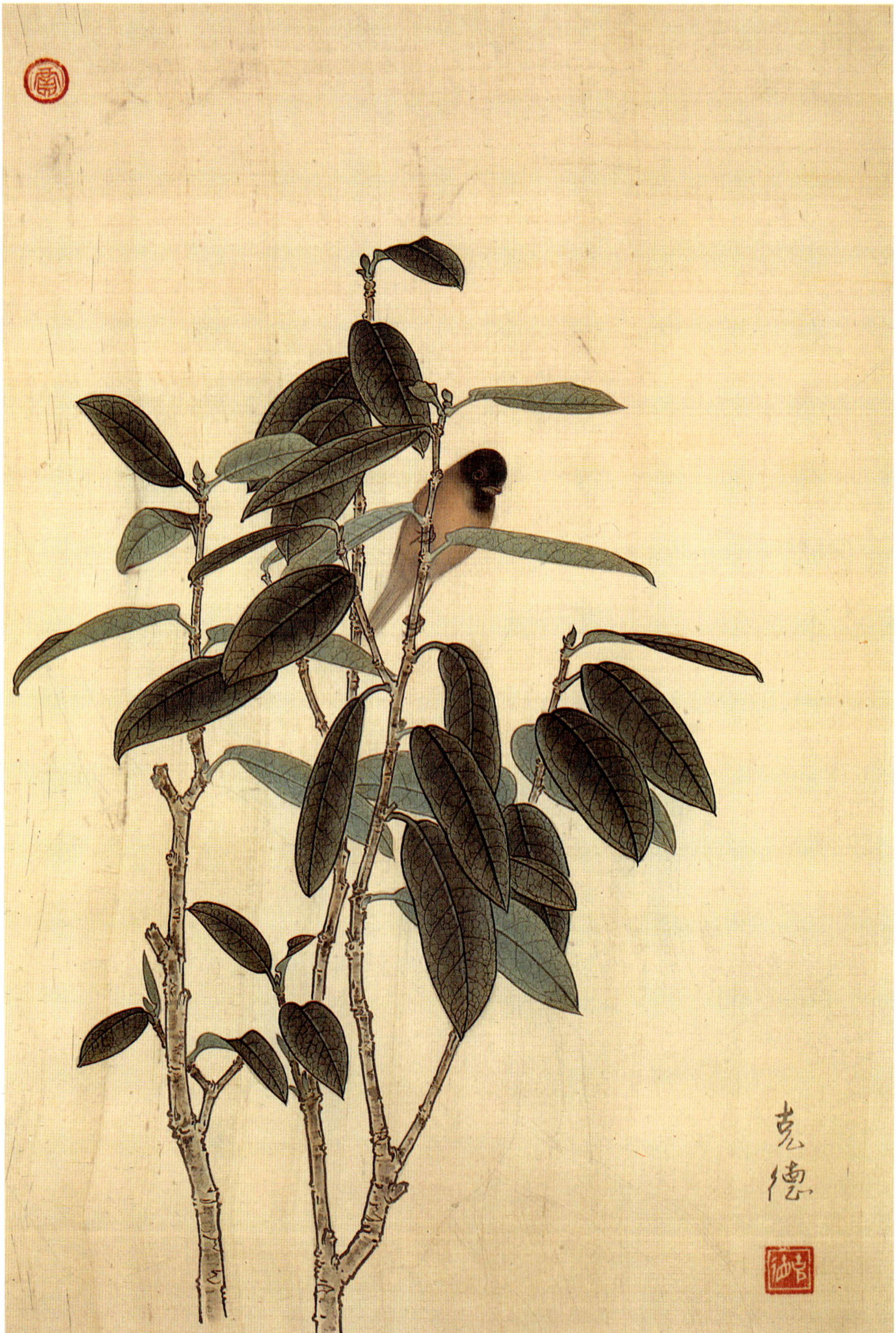

金 山 茶（1985） 绢本
Jinshan Tea
45 × 60cm (1985) on silk

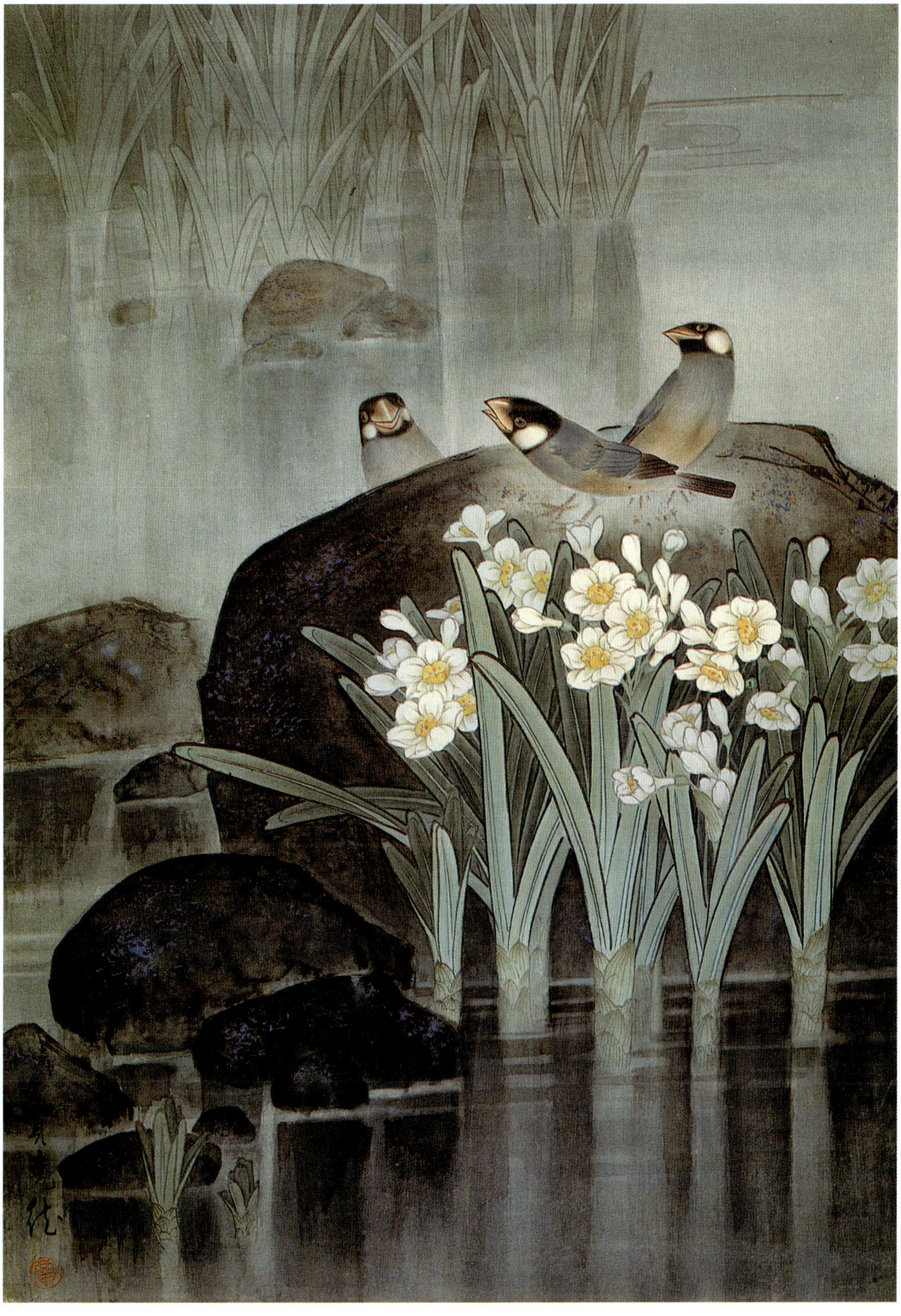

清　　露（1982）　纸本
Clear Dew
60 × 80cm (1982) on paper

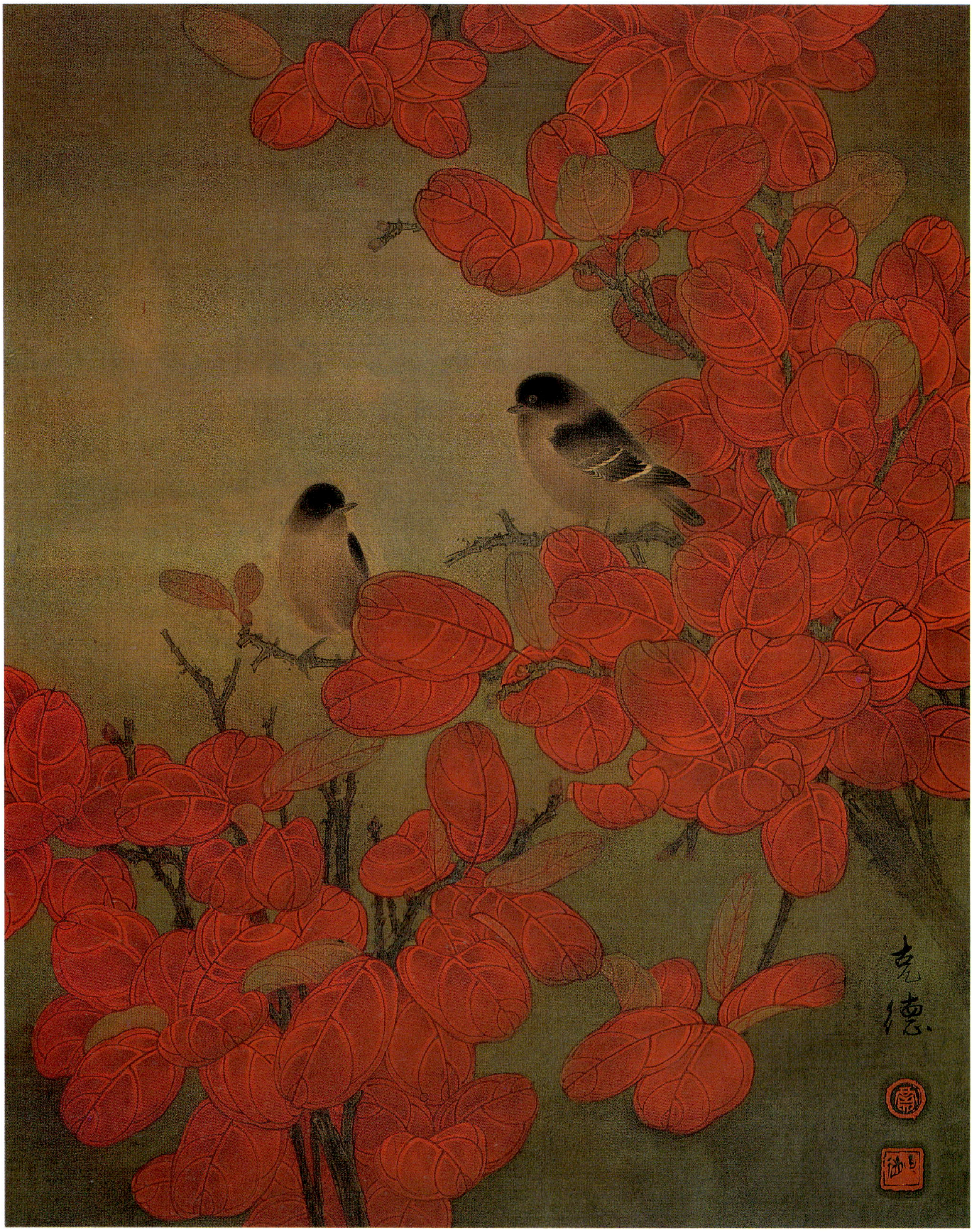

丹　　枫（1995）　绢本
Red Maple
45 × 60cm (1995) on silk

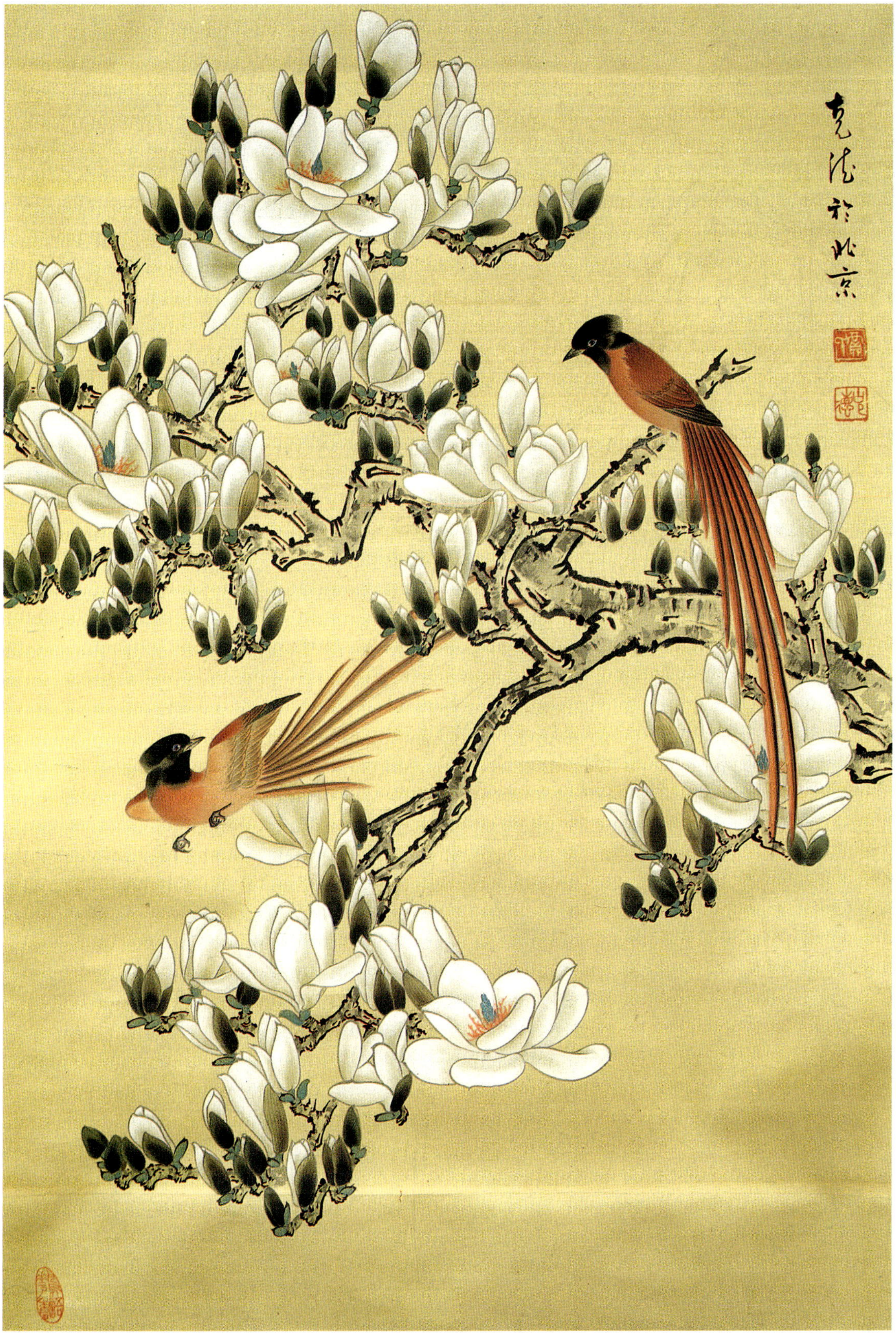

玉兰绶带（1978） 绢本
Magnolis and Birds
45 × 60cm (1978) on silk

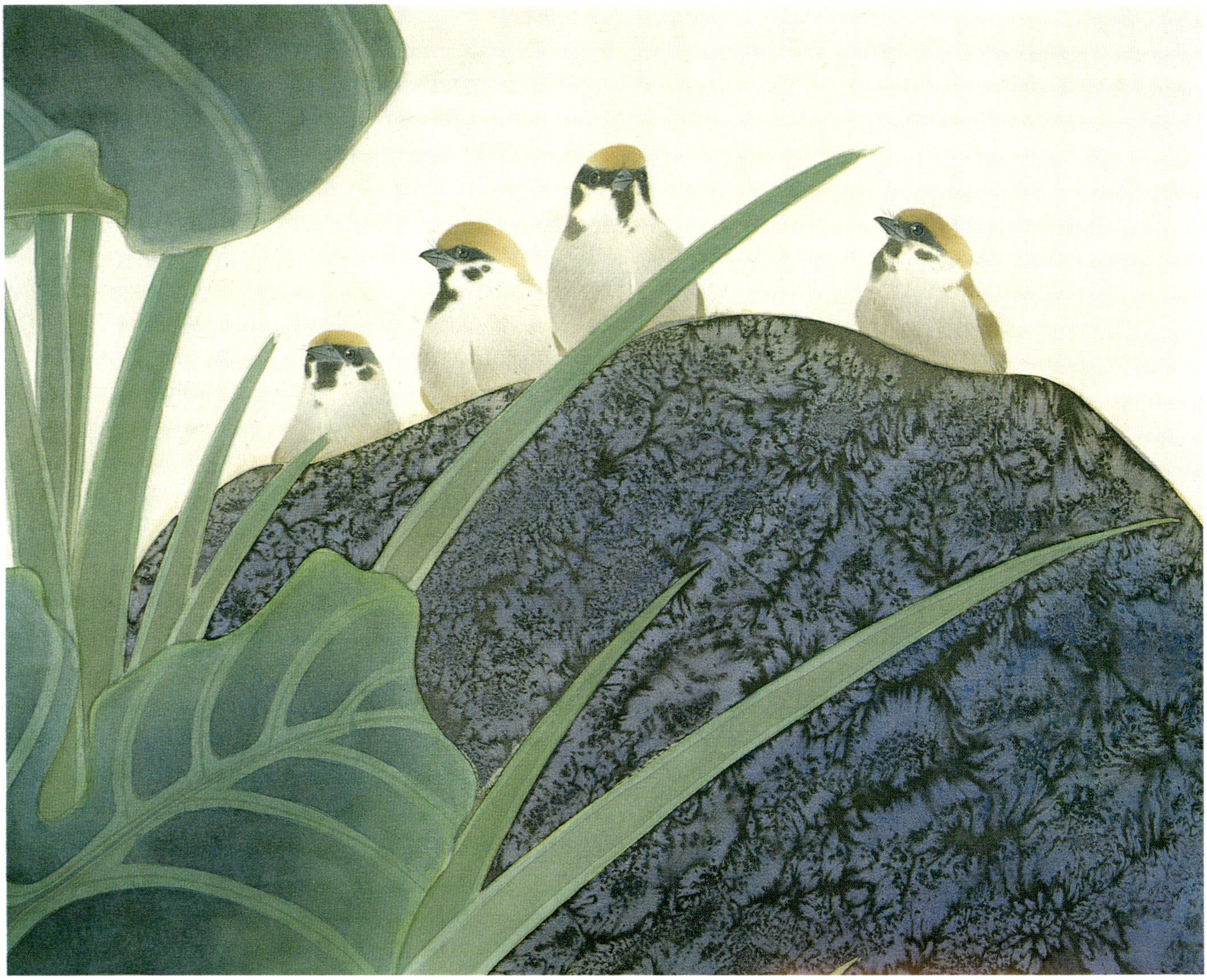

春色融融（局部）（1986）　绢本
Joyful Spring
50 × 80cm (1986) on silk (detail)

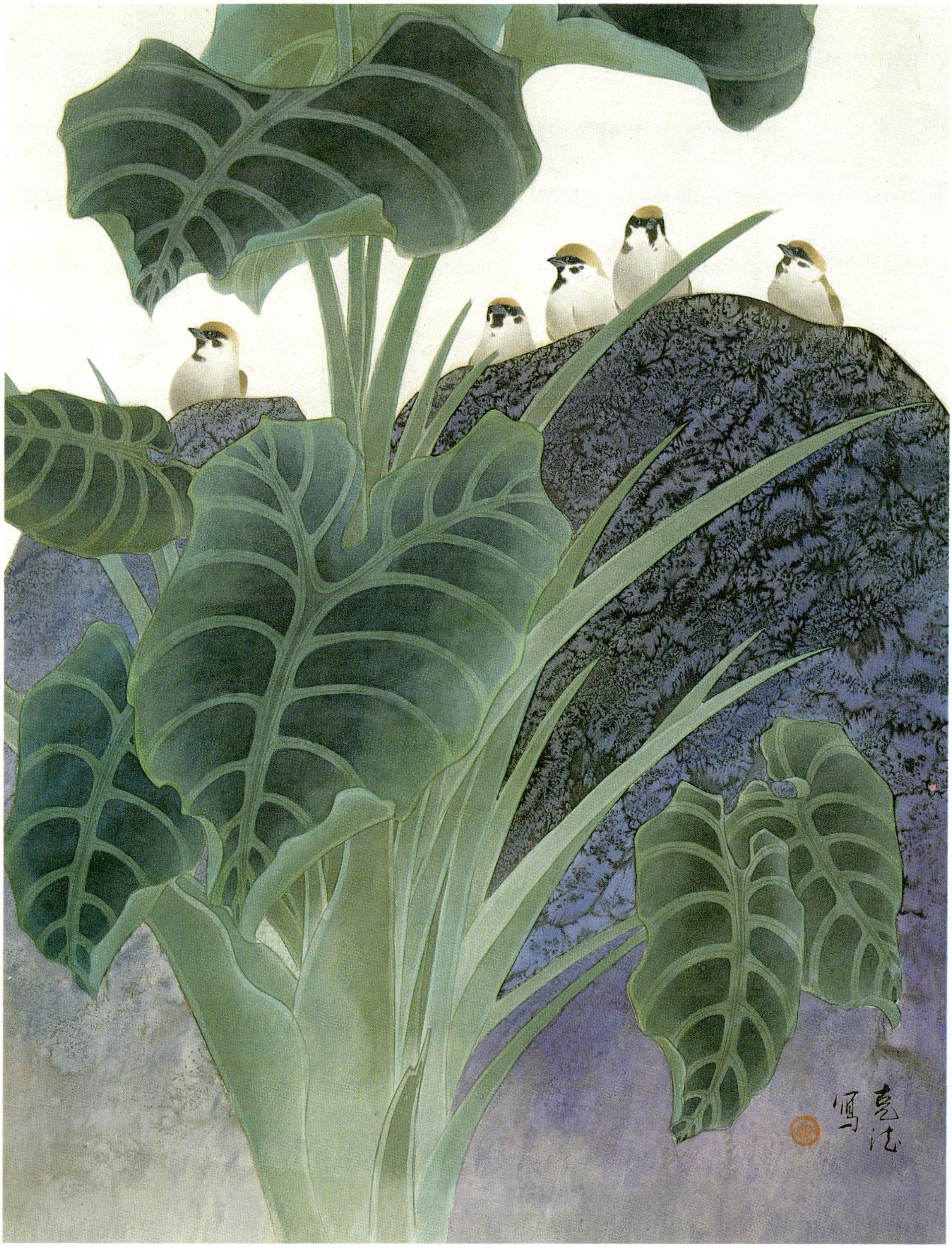

春色融融（1986） 绢本
Joyful Spring
50 × 80cm (1986) on silk

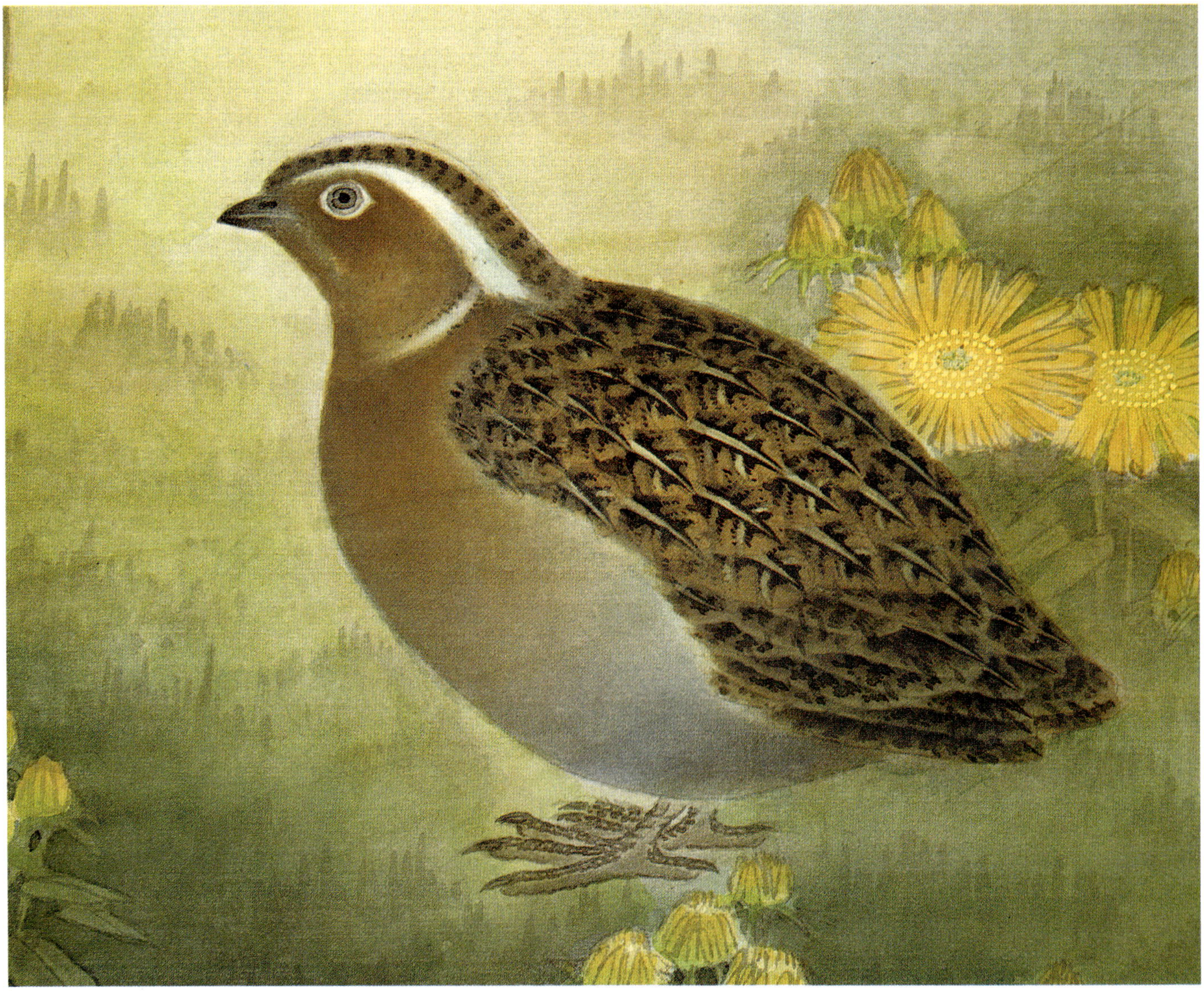

金盏玉蕊（局部）（1996） 绢本
Birds Amidst Blossoms
70 × 75cm (1996) on silk (detail)

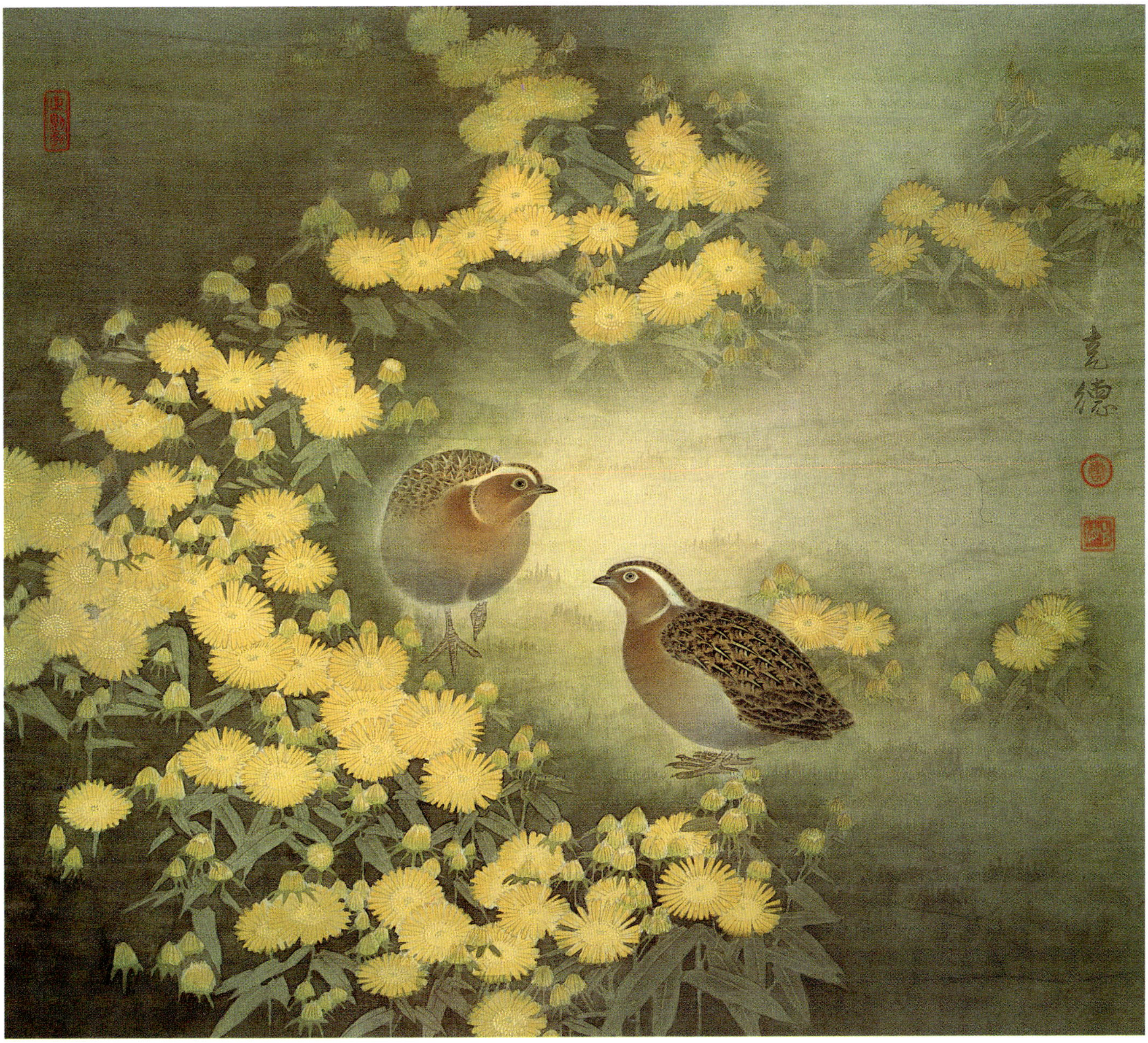

金盏玉蕊（1996） 绢本
Birds Amidst Blossoms
70 × 75cm (1996) on silk

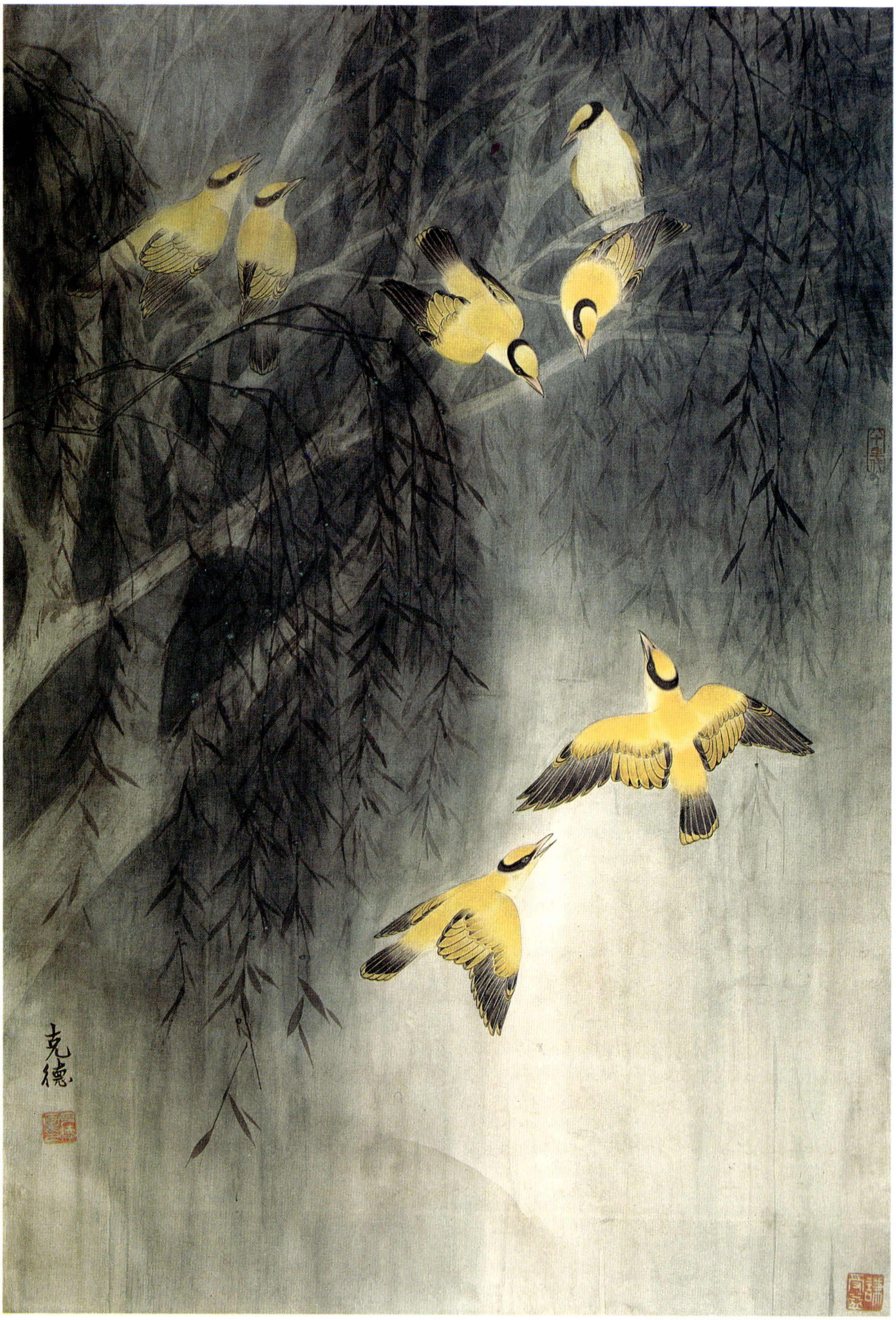

春晓闻莺（1983） 绢本
Orioles in Spring Morning
60 × 90cm (1983) on silk

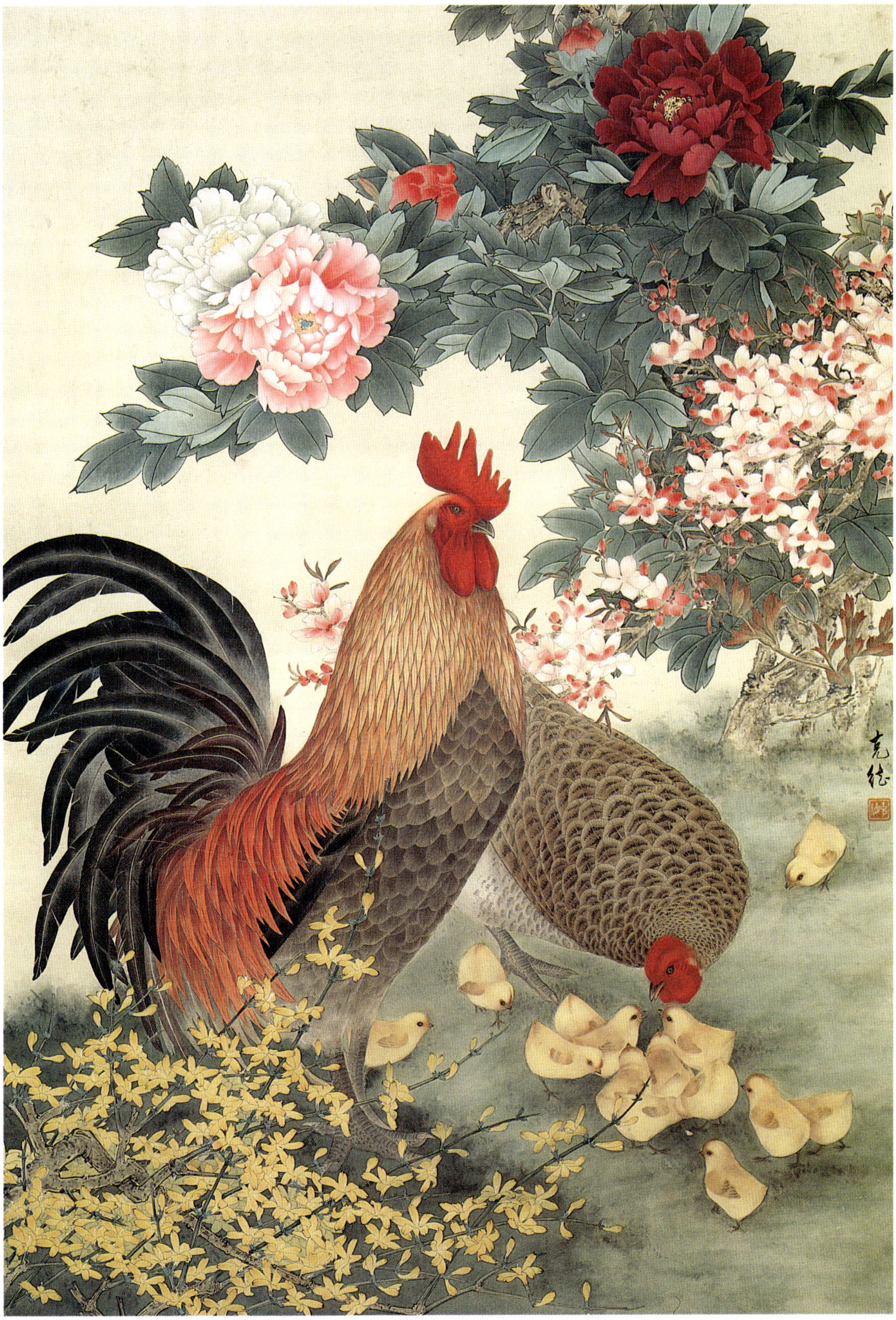

报 春 图（1982） 绢本
Spring Harbinger
80 × 130cm (1982) on silk

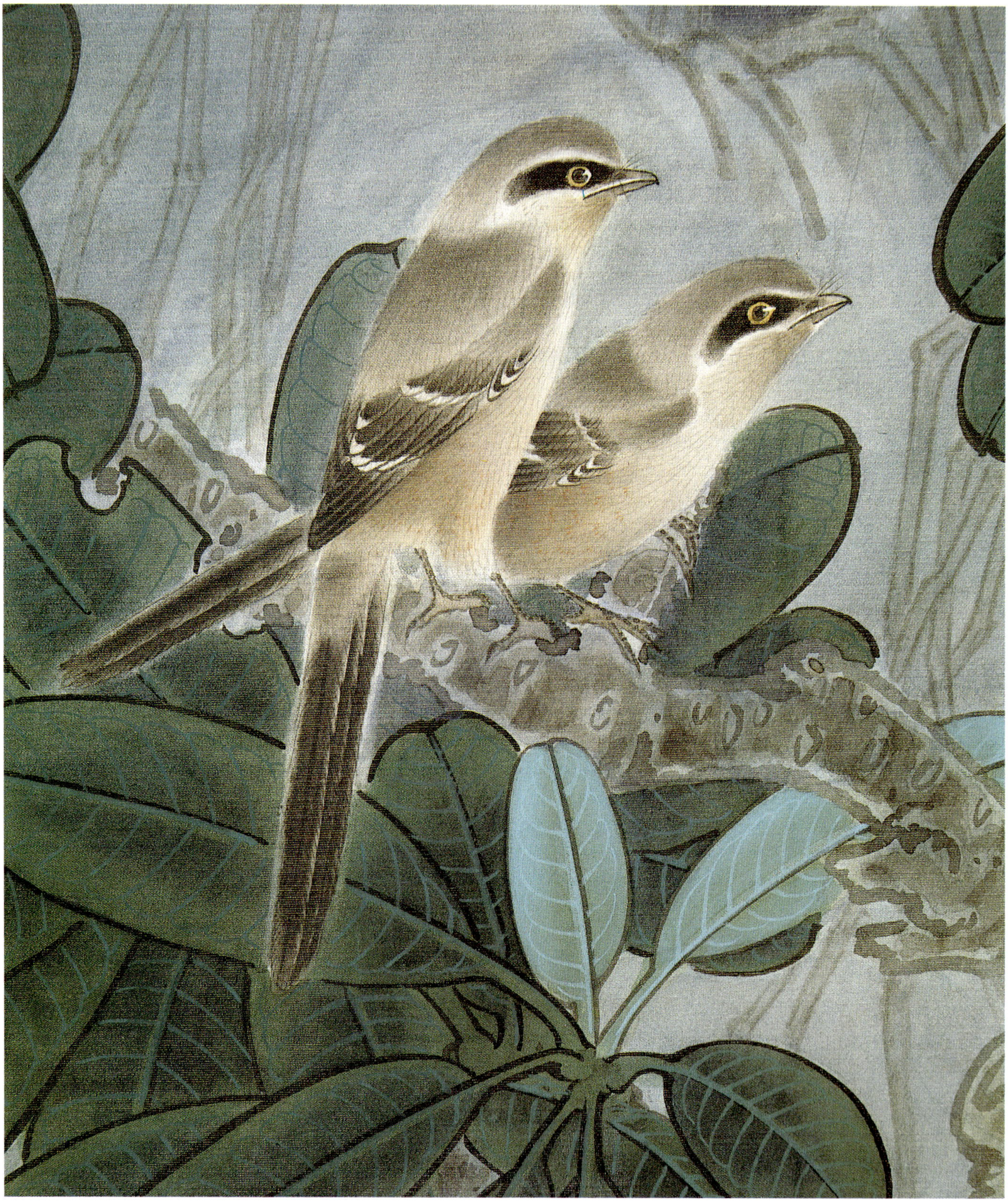

秀掩丛绿（局部）（1986） 绢本
Beauty Amidst Green
45 × 90cm (1986) on silk (detail)

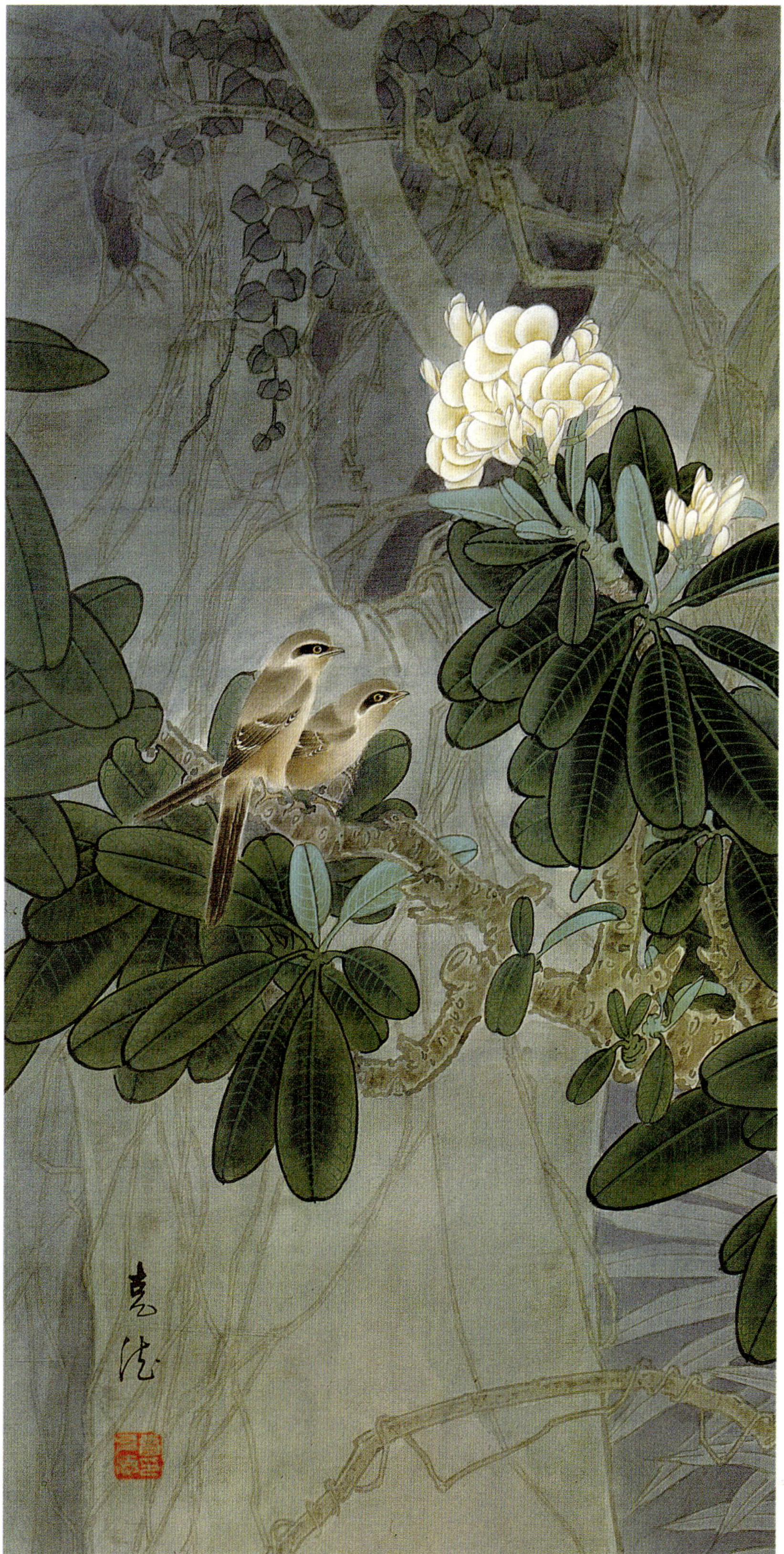

秀掩丛绿（1986） 绢本
Beauty Amidst Green
45 × 90cm (1986) on silk

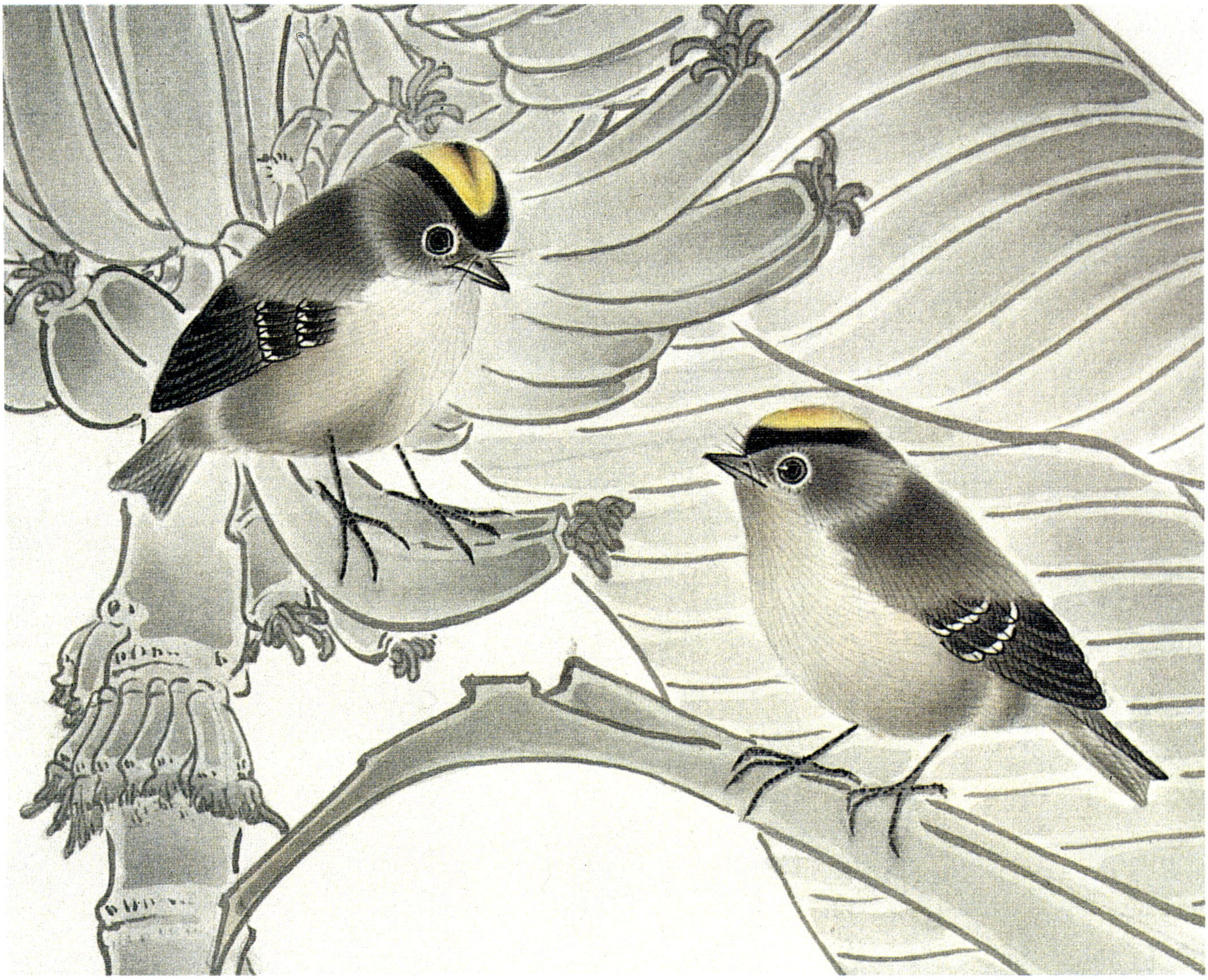

蕉　　荫（局部）（1986）　绢本
In the Shade of Palm
45×75cm (1986) on silk (detail)

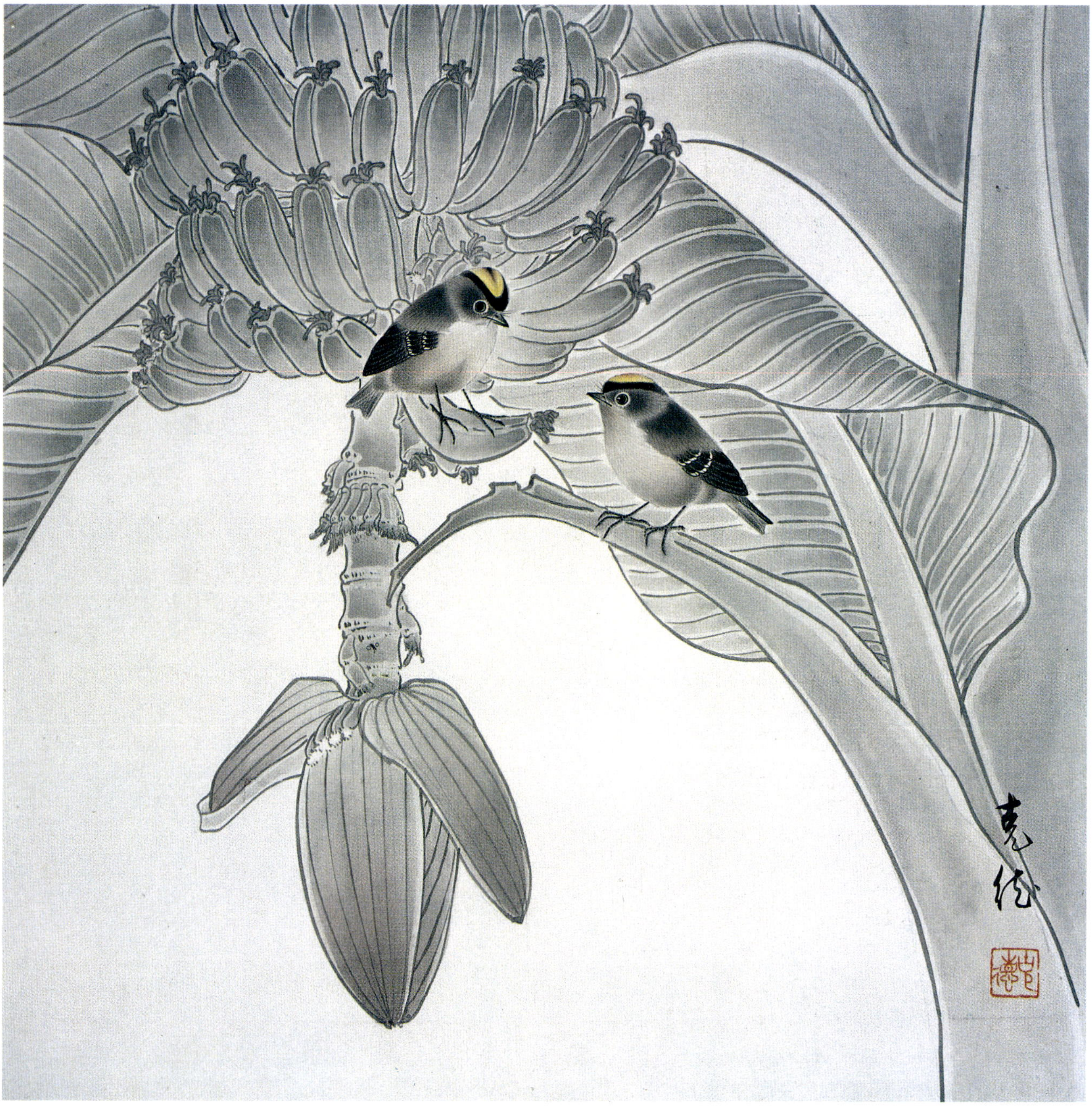

蕉　　荫（1986）绢本
In the Shade of Palm
45 × 75cm (1986) on silk

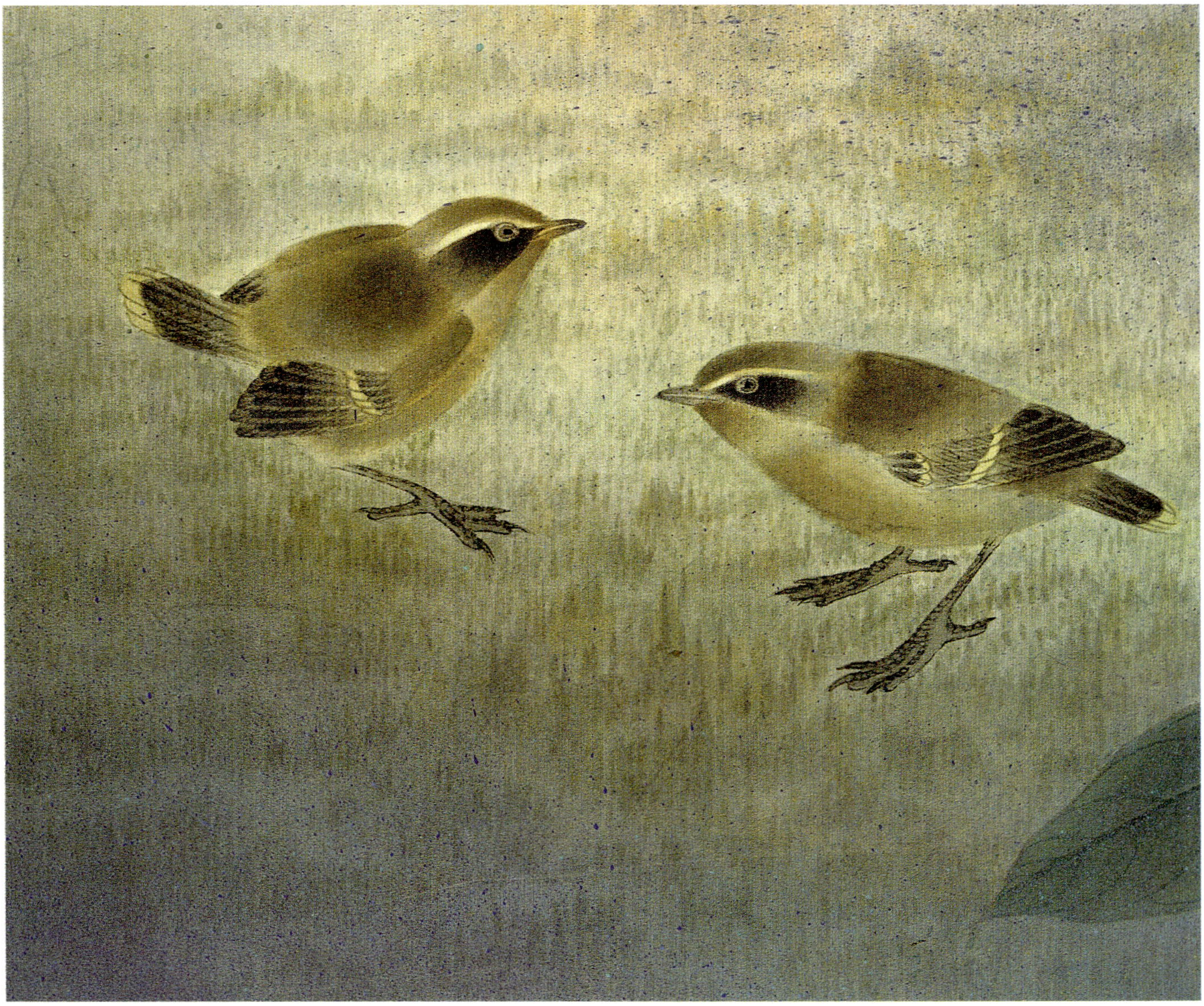

初　　霁（局部）（1996）　绢本
Shortly After Rain
75×80cm (1996) on silk (detail)

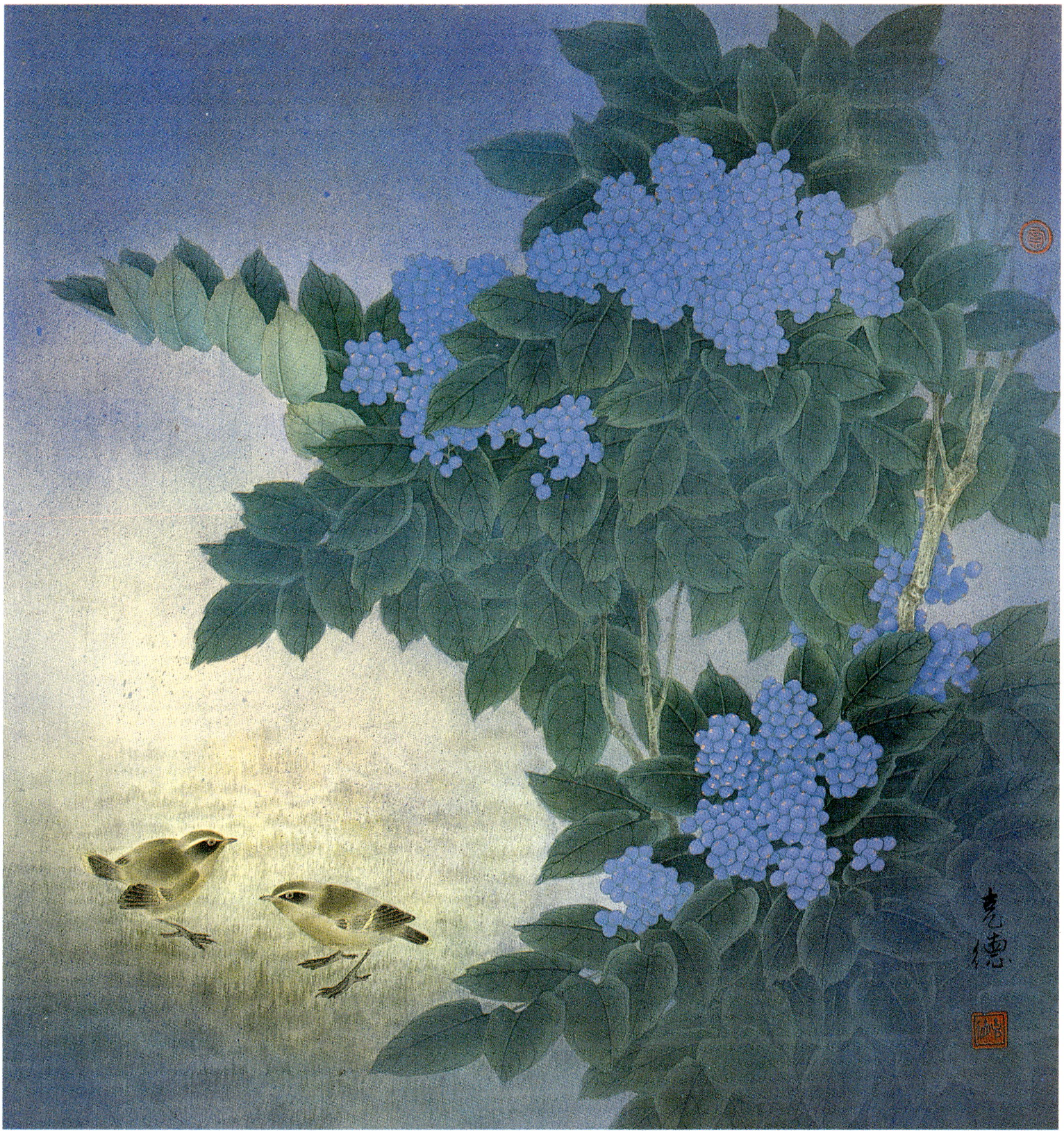

初　　霁（1996） 绢本
Shortly After Rain
75 × 80cm (1996) on silk

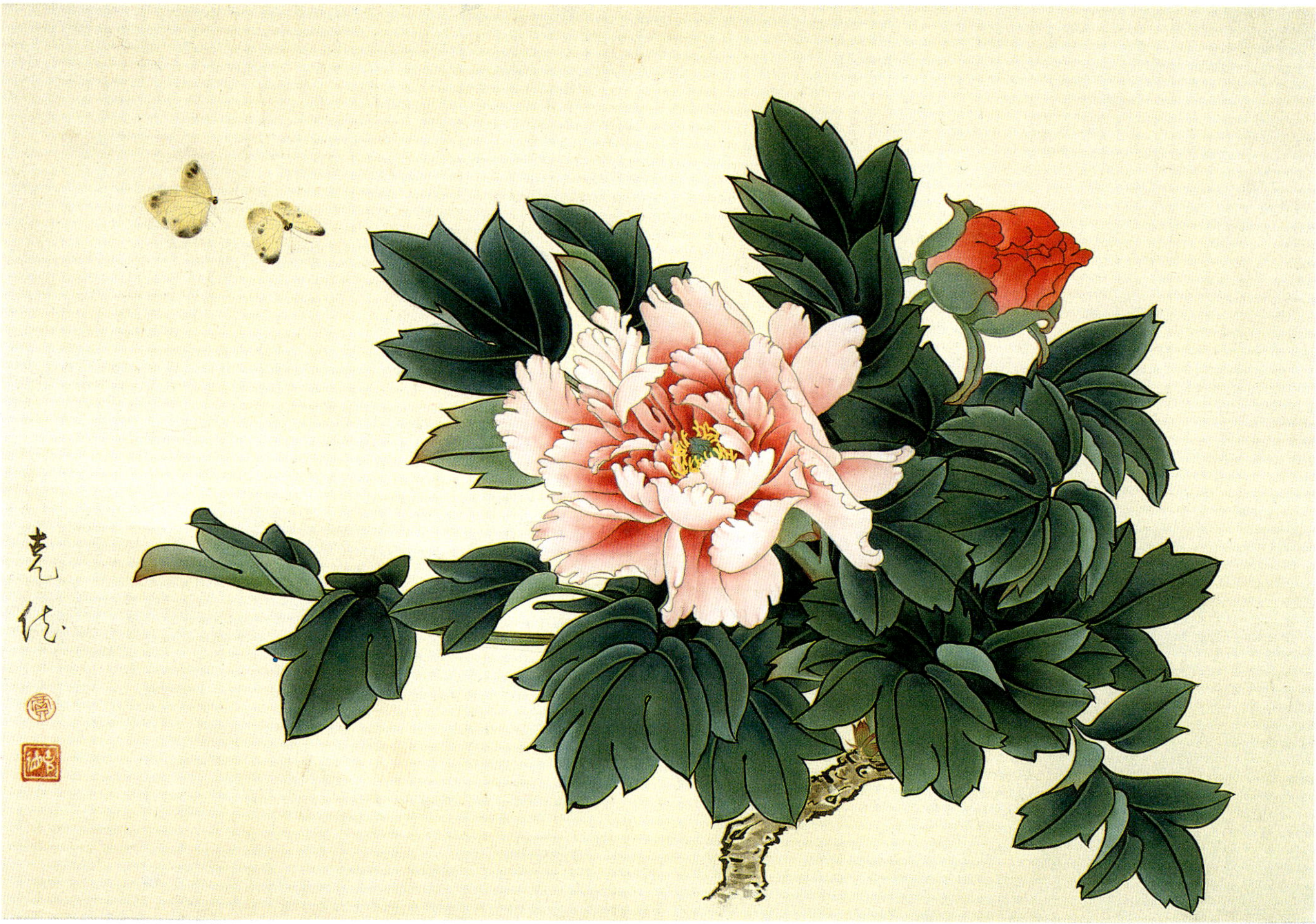

牡 丹（赵粉）（1982） 绢本
Peony (Zhao pink)
60 × 45cm (1982) on silk

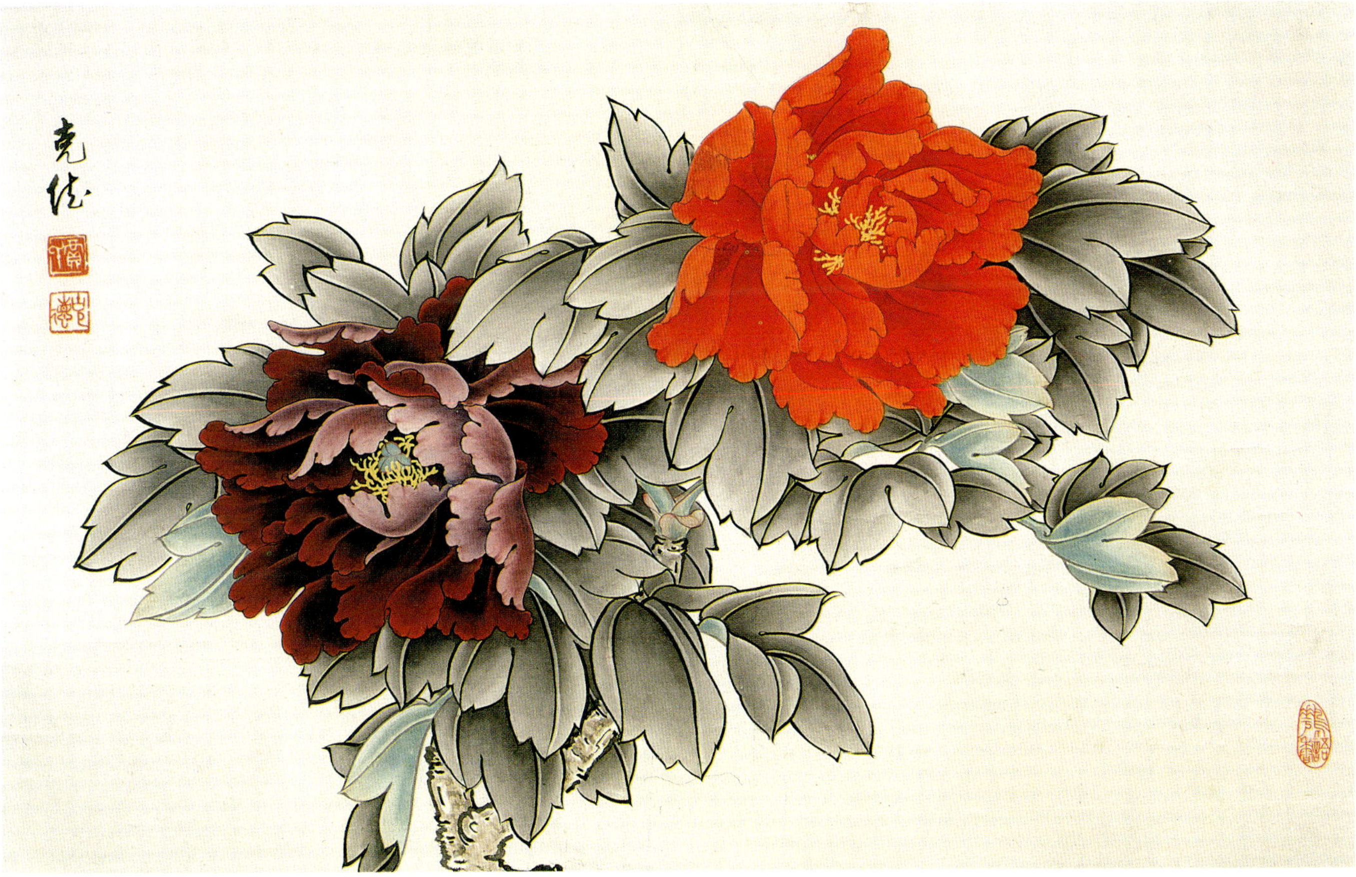

牡丹（魏紫）（1982） 纸本
Peony (Wei purple)
60 × 45cm (1982) on paper

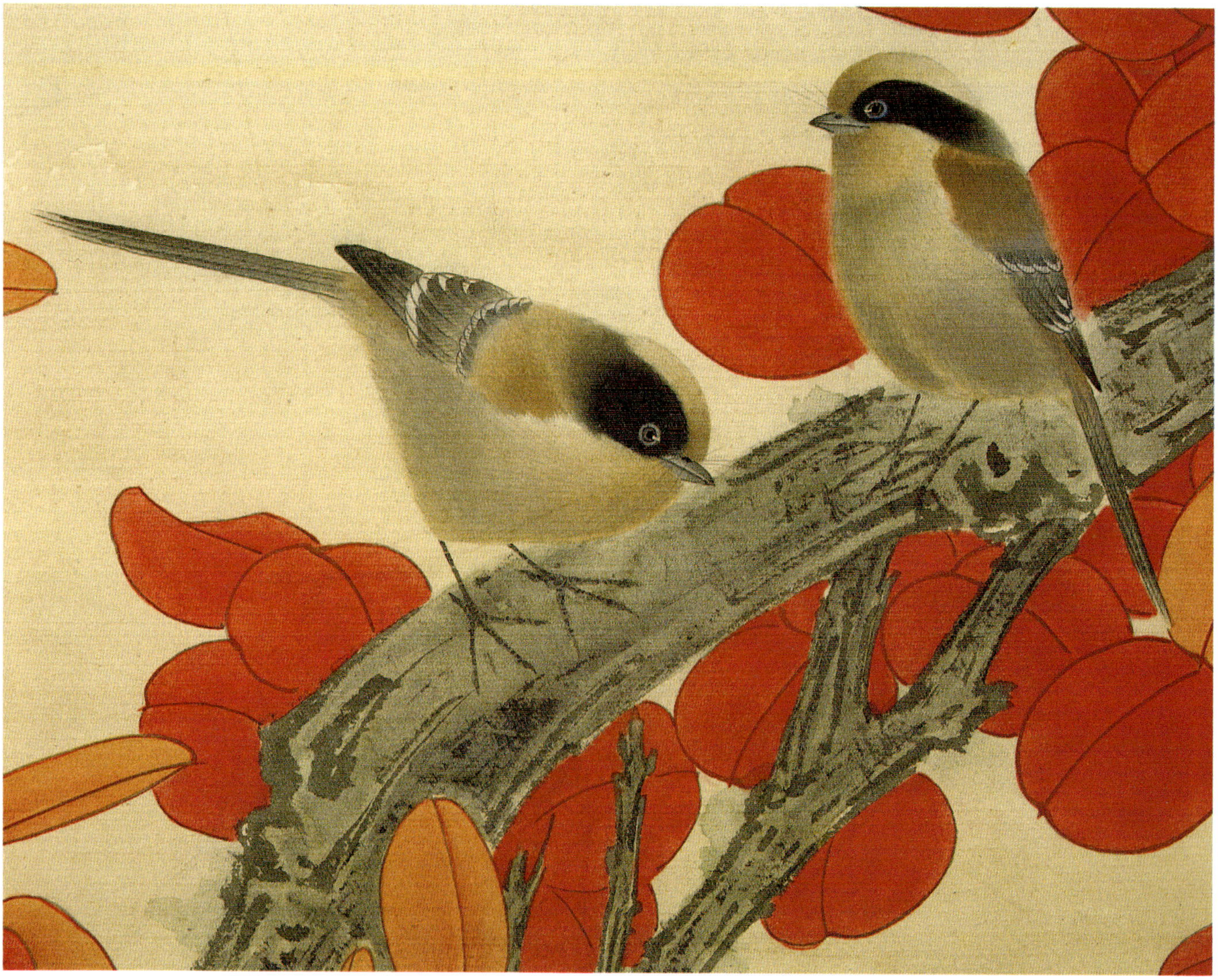

秋林红雨（局部）（1995） 绢本
Red Leaves in Autumn
50 × 80cm (1995) on silk (detail)

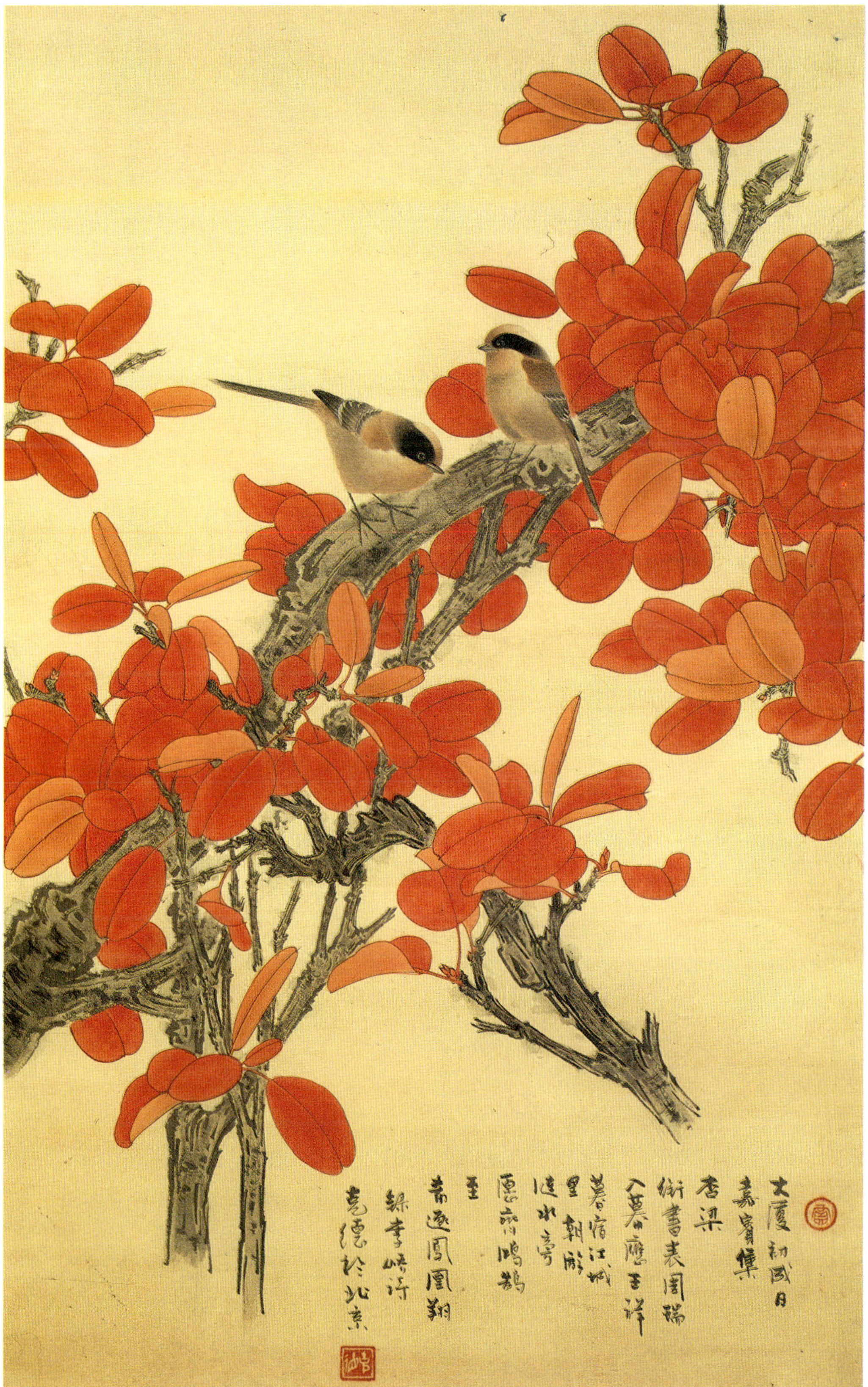

秋林红雨（1995） 绢本
Red Leaves in Autumn
50 × 80cm (1995) on silk

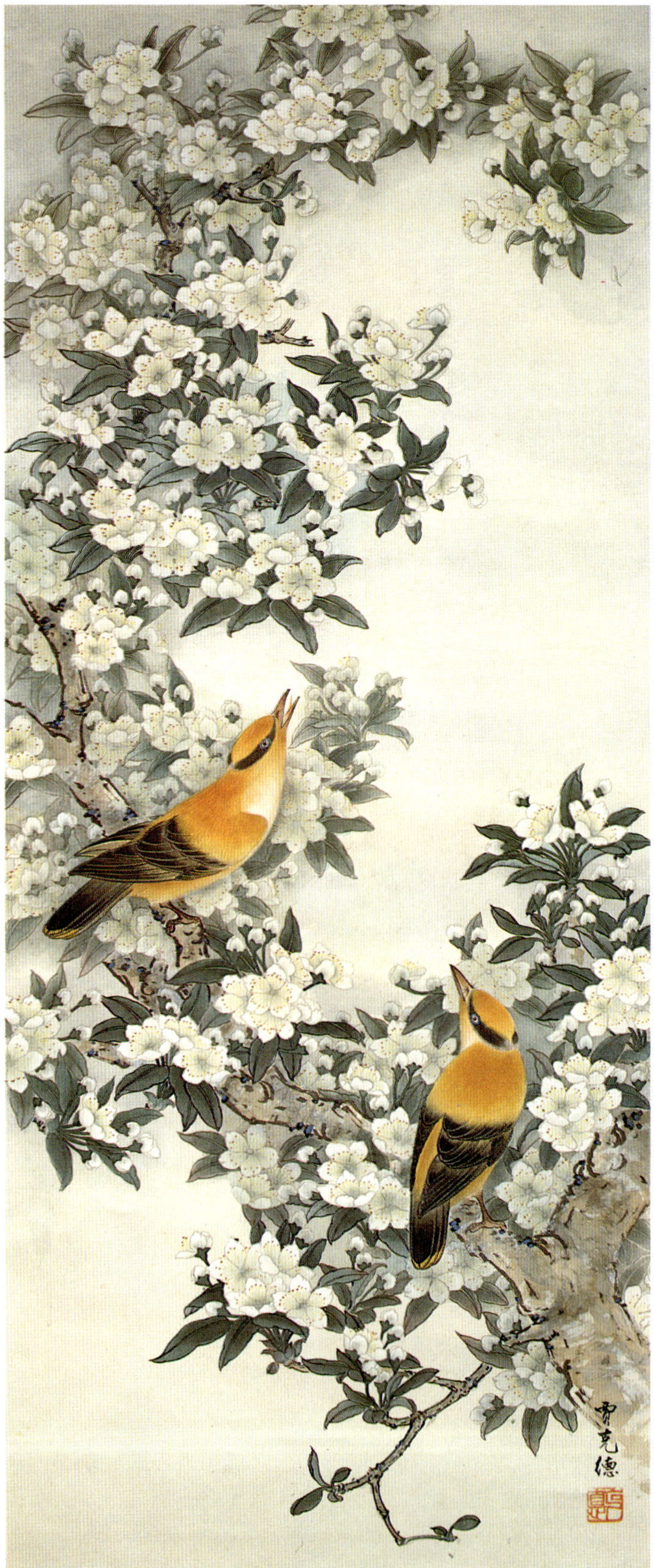

梨花黄鹂（1979） 绢本
Pear Blossoms and orioles
45 × 110cm (1979) on silk

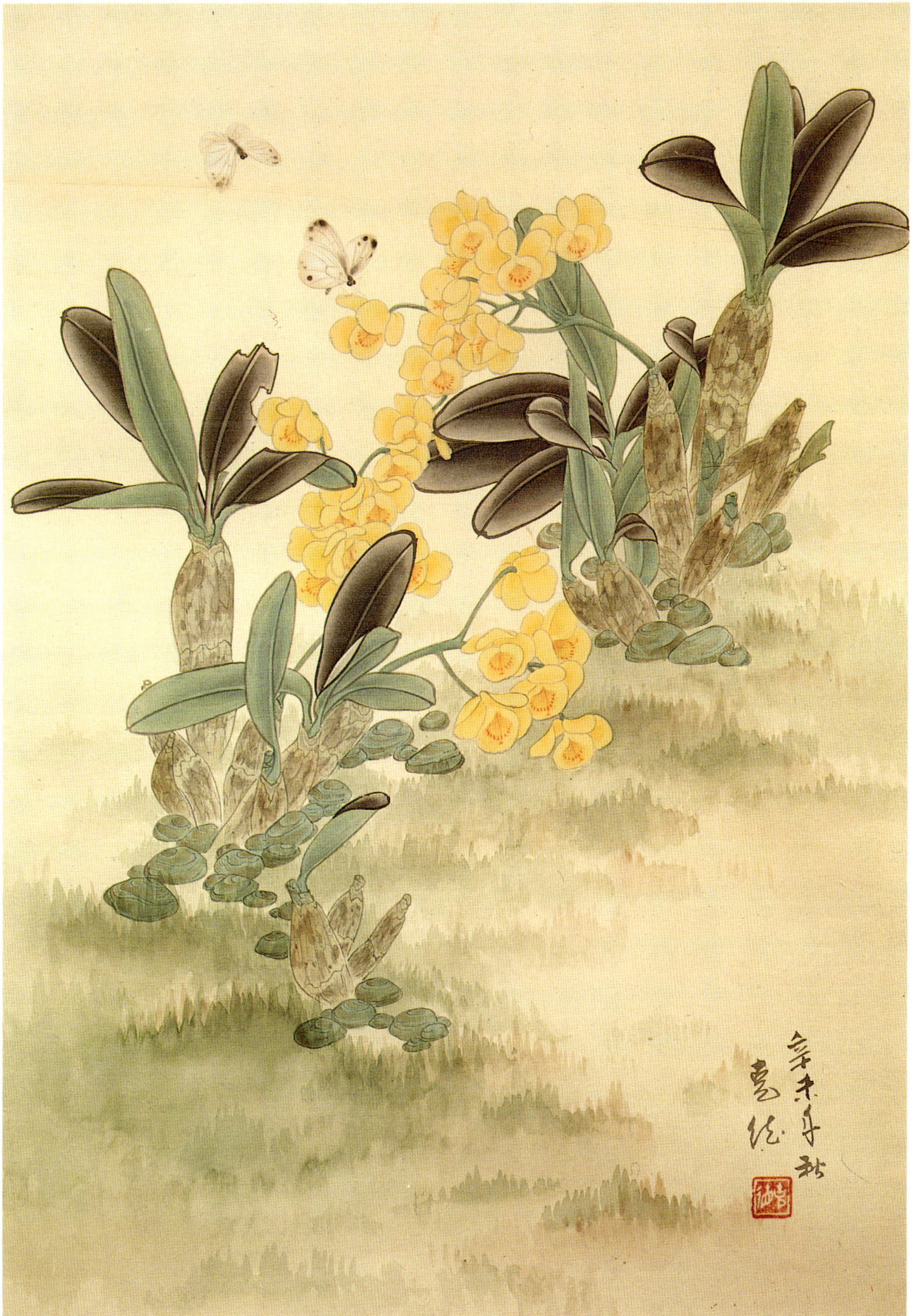

石　　斛（1994）　绢本
Wild Flowers
50 × 80cm (1994) on silk

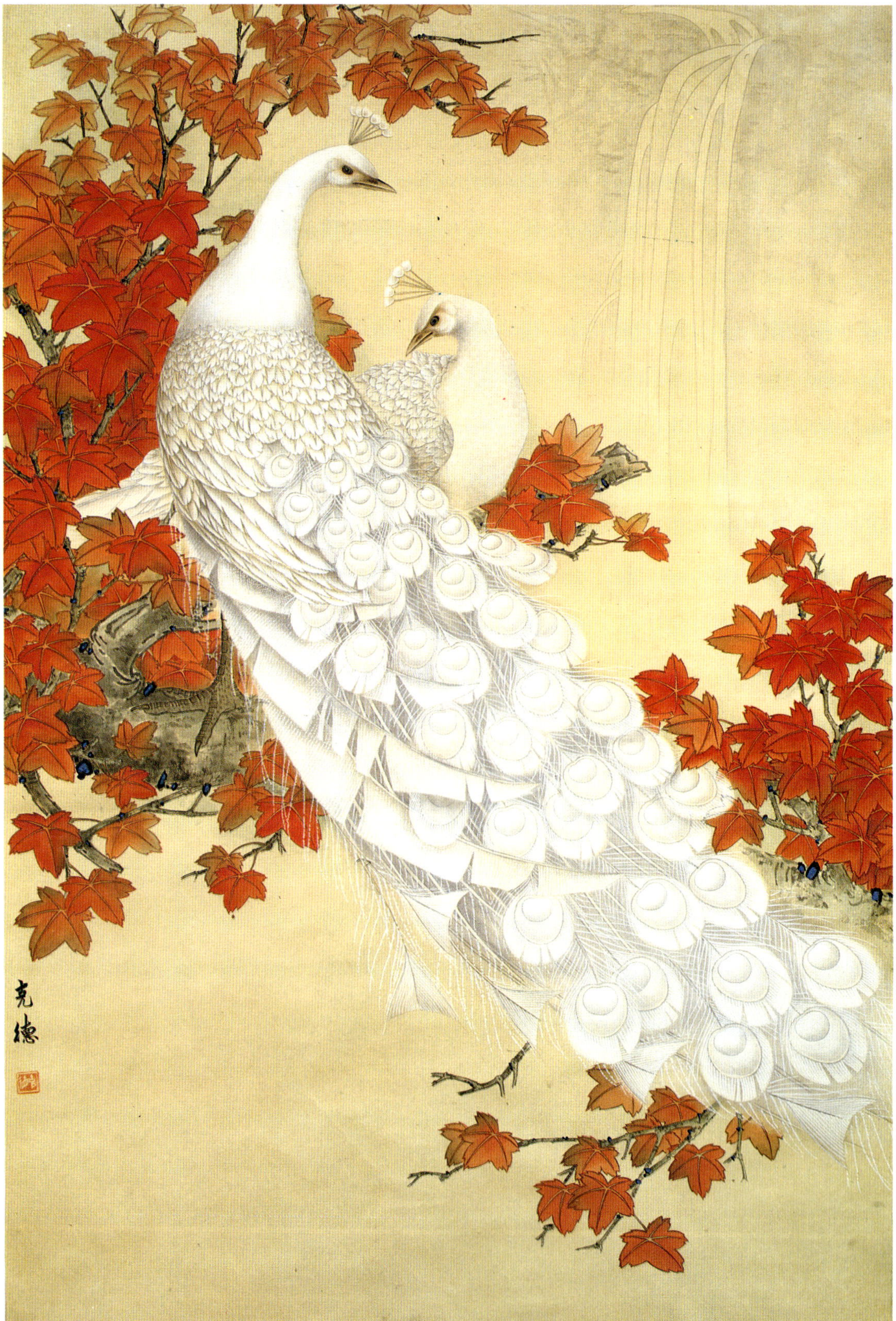

孔雀丹枫（1988） 绢本
Peacocks and Red Maples
80 × 130cm (1988) on silk

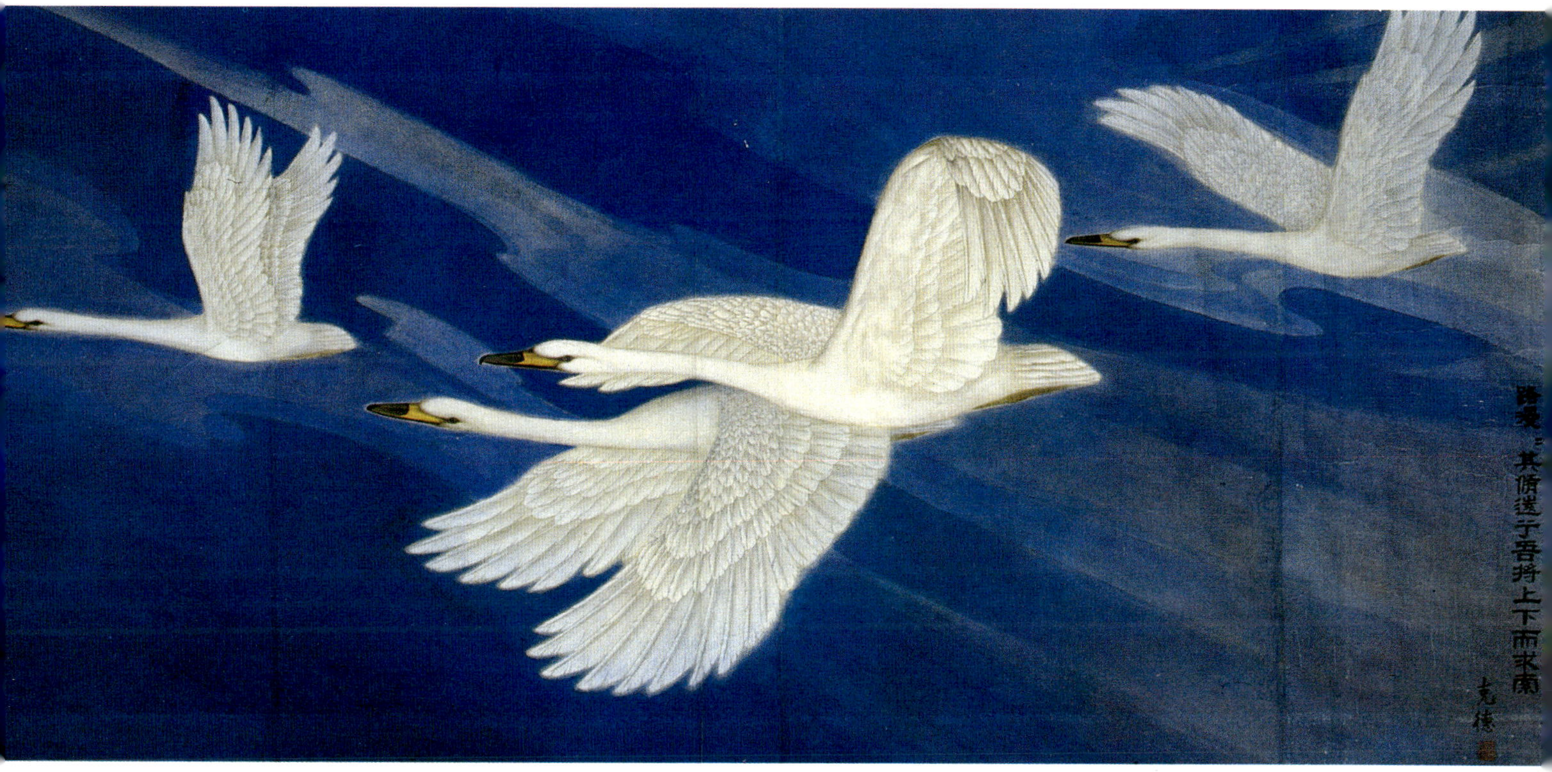

路 漫 漫（1982） 纸本
A Long Road
240 × 120cm (1982) on paper

目 录

CONTENTS

（京）新登字131号

图书在版编目（CIP）数据

贾克德工笔花鸟画集/贾克德绘；刘宗仁译. - 北京：中国世界语出版社，1997.5

Ⅰ.贾··· Ⅱ.①贾··· ②刘··· Ⅲ.工笔画：花鸟画 - 作品集 - 中国 - 现代 Ⅳ.J222.7

中国版本图书馆CIP数据核字（97）第07993号

编　　辑：曲维波、望天星
撰　　文：潘絜兹
翻　　译：刘宗仁
责任编辑：曲维波
装帧设计：傅桂生

贾克德工笔花鸟画集

*

中国世界语出版社出版
北京博诚印刷厂印刷
（北京1201工厂）
中国国际图书贸易总公司（国际书店）发行
（中国北京车公庄西路35号）
邮政信箱第399号　　邮政编码：100044
1997年5月（16开）第一版第一次印刷
ISBN 7－5052－0325－8／J.38（外）
05000
84－CE－775P